# GOD'S
## *Blessings*
### *for the*
# GRADUATE

BARBOUR BOOKS
An Imprint of Barbour Publishing, Inc.

# Contents

# GOD HAS SO MANY BLESSINGS
# IN STORE FOR YOU, GRAD!

*Congratulations!*
You've just achieved a major goal—graduation! All of your hard work has finally paid off and you definitely deserve a pat on the back. Good job.

Hopefully you know more today than you did when you started. An education is a great gift. It opens doors that would otherwise never be open. It gives us power to change our circumstances and can increase our influence with others. It provides us with myriad opportunities to change the world.

But have you noticed the more you learn, the more you realize how much more there is to learn? We could spend the rest of our lives going to school, and yet the knowledge we'd acquire would be just a drop in the vast ocean of all there is to know.

Karl Barth was one of the most influential theologians of the twentieth century. This highly educated man studied at some of the world's finest universities and wrote volumes of complex theological material. In 1962, Barth visited the United States, and someone asked him if he could sum up the essence of all he had written.

His reply?

"Jesus loves me, this I know, for the Bible tells me so."

Simple words, but their message is incredibly profound. No matter where life takes you, don't ever lose sight of the beauty and simplicity of the many blessings God gives us, His children, and the reminders of those promises in His Word—His gift to you for today and for the rest of your life.

# I Believe: Owning My Faith

My relationship with Jesus Christ is my end-all,
be-all. Without Christ in my life I would be nothing;
He is my strength, my rock, my fortress, and deliverer.
However, it wasn't until my freshman year of college when
I moved away from home and everyone that I knew that I
really came to fully and completely depend on God with
every breath that I took. Even though I was born and raised
in a Christian home and family setting, realizing that I
am not in control of my life is what allowed me to own
my faith. It also enabled me to have an active,
dependent relationship with God.

EMILY HOERNSCHEMEYER, 20

Whether you are heading to college or starting a new job,
your life will be different after graduation. Tossing that
cap into the air symbolized not only an ending, but also
a new beginning. As Dr. Seuss would say, "Oh, the places
you'll go!"

Graduation marks a milestone in your life and opens
up possibilities for you. It's exciting, but at the same time it
may be overwhelming to face so many choices and changes
at once. Now is the time to be sure you know what you
believe and truly own your faith.

Consider the difference between religion and
relationship. *Religion* is made up of traditions and doctrines,

while a *relationship* is personal, living, and growing. Which does God desire? Of course, as a loving heavenly Father, He longs to have a relationship with His children. He tells us to "be still, and know that I am God." We tend to forget the "be still" part, don't we? Life gets busy, but setting aside a quiet time to pray and read your Bible will strengthen your walk with God. It will help keep your thoughts and ways aligned with His.

Finding a church where you can worship and grow in the Lord is important. Most churches have groups that meet during the week for Bible study. Church is a great place to develop friendships with other believers.

Think about your passions and abilities. Are you musical or skilled in construction? Do you enjoy children? Serving at church or a mission organization is a great way to use your gifts to honor God. It's a lot of fun, and the blessings are great. Matthew 5:16 (NASB) says, "Let your light shine before men in such a way that they may see your good works, and glorify your Father who is in heaven." Service puts action to your faith and points others to God.

Uncertainties are a reality in life, but God has promised never to leave you. Jeremiah 29:11 (NIV) says that God's plans are to "prosper you and not to harm you." Own your faith, act on it, and give God control. Allow Him to sit in the driver's seat. Give Him the wheel. There will be some twists and turns in the road, but you can trust Him to get you where you are going.

When you feel down or depressed, do something for others. Visit an elderly relative, bake cookies for neighbors, or offer to babysit for friends so they can have an evening out on the town. This will shift your focus from your own problems to helping others.

*"Be still, and know that I am God; I will be exalted
among the nations, I will be exalted in the earth."*
PSALM 46:10 NIV

Start keeping a prayer journal. Record your
prayer requests as well as God's answers.

*For in the gospel a righteousness of God is revealed—
a righteousness that is by faith from first to last,
just as it is written: "The righteous will live by faith."*
ROMANS 1:17 NIV

*But the fruit of the Spirit is love, joy, peace, forbearance,
kindness, goodness, faithfulness, gentleness and self-control.
Against such things there is no law.*
GALATIANS 5:22–23 NIV

Keep some note cards with stamps and return address labels in your desk drawer. Write a note each week to a friend or relative. Include a scripture verse and a word of encouragement. Pray specifically for the needs of that person throughout the week.

◆

*I will praise God's name in song and glorify him with thanksgiving.*
PSALM 69:30 NIV

◆

Faith is a personal thing, intimate in nature. You cannot lean on another's faith or another's walk with Jesus. You must find your own faith in Christ.

◆

Purchase a devotional book to read during your daily quiet time with God. There are devotional books specifically designed for students, women, men, singles, etc.

◆

*We ought always to give thanks to God for you, brethren, as is only fitting, because your faith is greatly enlarged, and the love of each one of you toward one another grows ever greater.*
2 THESSALONIANS 1:3 NASB

*"But blessed is the man who trusts me, GOD, the woman who sticks with GOD. They're like trees replanted in Eden, putting down roots near the rivers—never a worry through the hottest of summers, never dropping a leaf, serene and calm through droughts, bearing fresh fruit every season."*

JEREMIAH 17:7–8 MSG

◆

To help you memorize scripture verses, write them on 3x5-inch index cards. Tape a card to your bathroom mirror, your car dashboard, or another prominent place. Practice it while getting ready in the morning or driving, etc., until you can say it from memory.

◆

*"You shall love the LORD your God with all your heart and with all your soul and with all your might."*

DEUTERONOMY 6:5 NASB

◆

*Consequently, faith comes from hearing the message, and the message is heard through the word about Christ.*

ROMANS 10:17 NIV

◆

*"All things are possible to him who believes."*

MARK 9:23 NKJV

# MAKING YOUR FAITH YOURS

*For you are all children of God*
*through faith in Christ Jesus.*
GALATIANS 3:26 NLT

◆

Pattie was raised in a Christian home. She grew up going to church every Sunday and rarely missed a youth group meeting. Her parents prayed with her and taught her to put God first in everything she did. Pattie went away to college knowing her mom and dad expected her to find a church home near her campus.

By the time school started, Pattie had no desire to attend church. For the first few Sunday mornings she slept in, and although she felt guilty, she just couldn't get excited about attending an unfamiliar church.

Things changed when Pattie got involved in a campus fellowship. She started going to a small group and gradually became more excited about living out her faith. Eventually she found a church she loved and looked forward to attending every Sunday. It wasn't necessarily her parents' idea of the perfect church, but it suited Pattie perfectly.

One of the challenges you'll face in this new phase of life is to make your faith your own. Your relationship with God may be shaped by your parents, but the next step for you to become a growing, active, and fruitful Christian is your responsibility. What steps can you take today to make your faith your own?

*I pray that you, being rooted and established in love, may*
*have power, together with all the Lord's holy people, to grasp*
*how wide and long and high and deep is the love of Christ,*
*and to know this love that surpasses knowledge—that you*
*may be filled to the measure of all the fullness of God.*

EPHESIANS 3:17–19 NIV

◆

Sign up for a Bible study class. Buy a brightly colored folder
to keep your notes in, and put the dates and times of the
class on your calendar. These tips will help you remember
to do the homework and show up for the study each week.

◆

*As the body without the spirit is dead,*
*so faith without deeds is dead.*

JAMES 2:26 NIV

◆

*Let us go right into the presence of God with sincere hearts*
*fully trusting him. For our guilty consciences have been*
*sprinkled with Christ's blood to make us clean, and our*
*bodies have been washed with pure water.*

HEBREWS 10:22 NLT

*We ask God to give you complete knowledge of his will and to give you spiritual wisdom and understanding. Then the way you live will always honor and please the Lord, and your lives will produce every kind of good fruit. All the while, you will grow as you learn to know God better and better.*

◆

*Then Jesus told him, "You believe because you have seen me. Blessed are those who believe without seeing me."*

JOHN 20:29 NLT

◆

I was on my own for the first time in my life, and college was a great season to search and discover what I believed for once. Finding a church that became a second family of mine was crucial in my relationship with the Lord during college. It's not easy because no one is "telling you to go to church or small group." But my soul longed to be a part of the body of Christ, and it opened many doors for questions from my nonbeliever friends.

MOLLY WEISGARBER, 22

*But without faith it is impossible to please Him,
for he who comes to God must believe that He is, and
that He is a rewarder of those who diligently seek Him.*

HEBREWS 11:6 NKJV

◆

*You never saw him, yet you love him. You still don't
see him, yet you trust him—with laughter and singing.
Because you kept on believing, you'll get what
you're looking forward to: total salvation.*

1 PETER 1:8–9 MSG

◆

*Watch, stand fast in the faith, be brave, be strong.*

1 CORINTHIANS 16:13 NKJV

◆

*Now faith is confidence in what we hope for
and assurance about what we do not see.*

HEBREWS 11:1 NIV

◆

*For you know that when your faith is tested,
your endurance has a chance to grow. So let it grow,
for when your endurance is fully developed, you will
be perfect and complete, needing nothing.*

JAMES 1:3–4 NLT

# God's Unending Love and Care

*"As the Father has loved me, so have I loved you.*
*Now remain in my love."*

JOHN 15:9 NIV

The perfect fairy-tale wedding had always been Krista's dream. She imagines herself adorned in a snow-white dress walking down the aisle, awash with rose petals. She is confident that if she waits long enough and patiently enough, her Prince Charming will come to give her the love she's always dreamed of.

What Krista doesn't know is that her future husband will never be able to love her just in the way she longs for. No spouse can. Many couples enter marriage believing that it's the beginning of an effortless happily-ever-after. They look to one another to fulfill their every need. It doesn't take long for disappointment and disillusionment to set in when their spouses fail to meet their expectations. These expectations are for a perfect love, and the truth is, no human being can love us the way God created us to be loved.

Only God can fill the void in our heart. When we learn to allow God's love to seep into our deepest places and fill our deepest needs, our human relationships are transformed. Instead of holding others to high and impossible expecta-tions, we are free to receive the love that they can offer us without being selfish and demanding, because we are allowing God to meet our deepest love needs.

*"For this is how God loved the world: He gave his one and only Son, so that everyone who believes in him will not perish but have eternal life."*

JOHN 3:16 NLT

◆

*Await the mercy of our Lord Jesus Christ, who will bring you eternal life. In this way, you will keep yourselves safe in God's love.*

JUDE 1:21 NLT

◆

*The LORD says, "Then I will heal you of your faithlessness; my love will know no bounds, for my anger will be gone forever."*

HOSEA 14:4 NLT

◆

*And I ask him that with both feet planted firmly on love, you'll be able to take in with all followers of Jesus the extravagant dimensions of Christ's love. Reach out and experience the breadth! Test its length! Plumb the depths! Rise to the heights! Live full lives, full in the fullness of God.*

EPHESIANS 3:17–19 MSG

◆

*"I'll be with you as you do this, day after day after day, right up to the end of the age."*

MATTHEW 28:20 MSG

*For I am convinced that neither death nor life,
neither angels nor demons, neither the present nor the future,
nor any powers, neither height nor depth, nor anything else
in all creation, will be able to separate us from the love
of God that is in Christ Jesus our Lord.*

ROMANS 8:38–39 NIV

◆

*GOD, your God, is above all a compassionate God.
In the end he will not abandon you, he won't bring you
to ruin, he won't forget the covenant with your
ancestors which he swore to them.*

DEUTERONOMY 4:31 MSG

◆

*And hope does not put us to shame, because God's
love has been poured out into our hearts through
the Holy Spirit, who has been given to us.*

ROMANS 5:5 NIV

◆

*And we have known and believed the love that
God has for us. God is love, and he who abides
in love abides in God, and God in him.*

1 JOHN 4:16 NKJV

*But you, O God, are both tender and kind, not easily angered, immense in love, and you never, never quit.*
PSALM 86:15 MSG

◆

*But God demonstrates his own love for us in this: While we were still sinners, Christ died for us.*
ROMANS 5:8 NIV

◆

*What marvelous love the Father has extended to us! Just look at it—we're called children of God! That's who we really are.*
1 JOHN 3:1 MSG

◆

*The LORD passed in front of Moses, calling out, "Yahweh! The LORD! The God of compassion and mercy! I am slow to anger and filled with unfailing love and faithfulness."*
EXODUS 34:6 NLT

◆

*God showed how much he loved us by sending his one and only Son into the world so that we might have eternal life through him. This is real love—not that we loved God, but that he loved us and sent his Son as a sacrifice to take away our sins.*
1 JOHN 4:9-10 NLT

# GOD PROVIDES FOR ME

*"Give us today our daily bread."*
MATTHEW 6:11 NIV

◆

Most of us don't really know what it means to rely on God for our daily bread. Our kitchen shelves are usually well-stocked with food—enough to carry us through the week if not through a month or two. Even when we feel like there's "nothing to eat in the house" we could probably rustle up a pretty decent meal with a little bit of effort. Yet in the book of Matthew, Jesus teaches us to pray for our daily bread.

The Israelites would have had a much clearer understanding of the concept of daily bread. In Exodus 16, when they complained of their discomfort and hunger in the desert, God explained that He would "rain down bread from heaven" (Exodus 16:4 NIV). The people were instructed to only gather what they would need for the day—anything more would spoil. Those who didn't follow God's instructions and tried to save some for the next morning ended up with a tent full of maggots. There are three principles we can learn from this story.

1. We can trust God to provide for our daily needs.
2. God's provision is enough—it is not necessary to hoard His blessings.
3. Relying on His provision frees us to think about other, more important, things.

God promises to provide your daily bread. You can trust Him to do it.

*"But the very hairs of your head are all numbered. Do not fear therefore; you are of more value than many sparrows."*

LUKE 12:7 NKJV

❖

*Whatever is good and perfect is a gift coming down to us from God our Father, who created all the lights in the heavens. He never changes or casts a shifting shadow. He chose to give birth to us by giving us his true word. And we, out of all creation, became his prized possession.*

JAMES 1:17–18 NLT

❖

*And the house of Israel called its name Manna. And it was like white coriander seed, and the taste of it was like wafers made with honey.*

EXODUS 16:31 NKJV

❖

*Those who know your name trust in you, for you, LORD, have never forsaken those who seek you.*

PSALM 9:10 NIV

❖

*And my God will meet all your needs according to the riches of his glory in Christ Jesus.*

PHILIPPIANS 4:19 NIV

*"What I'm trying to do here is to get you to relax,
to not be so preoccupied with getting, so you can respond
to God's giving. People who don't know God and the way he
works fuss over these things, but you know both God and how
he works. Steep your life in God-reality, God-initiative, God-
provisions. Don't worry about missing out. You'll find all
your everyday human concerns will be met."*

MATTHEW 6:31–33 MSG

◆

*[God] guards you when you leave and when you return,
he guards you now, he guards you always.*

PSALM 121:8 MSG

◆

*Abraham named the place Yahweh-Yireh (which means "the
LORD will provide"). To this day, people still use that name as
a proverb: "On the mountain of the LORD it will be provided."*

GENESIS 22:14 NLT

◆

*And my God shall supply all your need according
to His riches in glory by Christ Jesus.*

PHILIPPIANS 4:19 NKJV

◆

*Those who seek the LORD shall not lack any good thing.*

PSALM 34:10 NKJV

*Keep falsehood and lies far from me; give me neither*
*poverty nor riches, but give me only my daily bread.*
PROVERBS 30:8 NIV

*He gave food to those who fear him,*
*he remembered to keep his ancient promise.*
PSALM 111:5 MSG

*"Your Father knows what you need before you ask him."*
MATTHEW 6:8 NIV

*He rained down showers of manna to eat,*
*he gave them the Bread of Heaven.*
PSALM 78:24 MSG

*You sent your good Spirit to instruct them, and you did not*
*stop giving them manna from heaven or water for their thirst.*
NEHEMIAH 9:20 NLT

*"And don't be concerned about what to eat and*
*what to drink. Don't worry about such things."*
LUKE 12:29 NLT

# New Digs:
## Adjusting to Different Surroundings

The key to adjusting to a new living situation
is trusting and depending on God.
When I moved into college my freshman year,
He was my comfort, my best friend,
and the one constant in my life.

EMILY HOERNSCHEMEYER, 20

You were probably comfortable in your surroundings before graduation. Do you find yourself in a new place now? Everything familiar has been replaced with the unknown. Whether you are living in a dorm, an apartment, or a house, with or without roommates, new surroundings can be unsettling. You were used to the creaks in the floor and the drip of the bathroom sink, but there are different noises to adjust to in this new place. Before long, you won't even notice them, but it may take awhile for this to feel like home.

View your new environment as an opportunity! Get out and see what is in the community. Have you located a post office yet? A grocery store? What about a local hole-in-the-wall restaurant? Ask around about fun things to do in the area. Introduce yourself to your neighbors. Get online and search for churches. Choose to find a church right away to get off to a great start. Whatever you do the first weekend you are there will dictate your future patterns.

You will probably be tempted to return to your "old turf" often during the first months. Of course, you don't want to lose touch with family and friends. Keep in mind, though, that you will only get out of your new community as much as you are willing to put into it. What does that mean? It means you need to make a conscious effort to build a life where you are. You may be in a big city or a small town. Both have their advantages. Take in the culture of this new place, whether that means visiting art museums, touring old homes, or maybe just trying out all the barbeque joints and picking a favorite.

Seek out places to meet new people while doing things that you enjoy. Join a gym or sports league. Volunteer at a local homeless shelter, nursing home, or library. If you are a student, many campuses have Christian student unions and student government groups that may interest you. You can also make friends quickly through your church by becoming a part of a weeknight community group or Bible study.

Remember that Jesus experienced the ultimate in adjusting to a new environment. He left heaven's glory for a fallen world and died to save us from sin. He left a throne for a manger bed and gave up angels' praise for carpentry. He knows about change! Have you asked Him to help you to feel comfortable in your new digs?

*Thank You, Lord, for this experience and for my
new surroundings. Help me to feel at home, adjust easily,
and make some new friends. Please provide me
with opportunities to reach out to others with
Your love in this place. Amen.*

Go to church the first Sunday you are living in a new place. You may wish to visit several churches, but set a goal to choose one and join within six weeks to get plugged into a local body of believers as soon as possible.

◆

*"And the Lord, He is the One who goes before you. He will be with you, He will not leave you nor forsake you; do not fear nor be dismayed."*
Deuteronomy 31:8 NKJV

◆

Change is invigorating. If the caterpillar stayed inside the chrysalis, never daring to break out of its comfort zone, the world would have no butterflies. Don't fear change. Embrace it!

◆

Be open to new friends in this new place who are not exactly like you or the friends you have had in the past. Certainly it is good to have some things in common with a friend, but he or she does not have to fit a certain mold.

*If I rise on the wings of the dawn, if I settle on the far side of the sea, even there your hand will guide me, your right hand will hold me fast.*

PSALM 139:9–10 NIV

◆

Do something each week that will help you become more comfortable in your new environment. Put it on the calendar and follow through with it. Many people procrastinate, allowing months to pass before they establish themselves in a new place.

◆

*Yea, though I walk through the valley of the shadow of death, I will fear no evil: for thou art with me; thy rod and thy staff they comfort me.*

PSALM 23:4 KJV

◆

*The LORD will protect you from all evil; He will keep your soul. The LORD will guard your going out and your coming in from this time forth and forever.*

PSALM 121:7–8 NASB

◆

Take some time to just drive around and check out the new area. Sometimes getting a little lost is the perfect way to figure out your way around.

After you have adjusted to your new home and feel more comfortable, do not forget how it felt to be the "new kid." Reach out to others. Welcome new students or coworkers. Take some cookies to a new neighbor.

◆

*The Lord's curse is on the house of the wicked,*
*but he blesses the home of the righteous.*
PROVERBS 3:33 NIV

◆

Keep your thoughts and feelings about the changes you are going through and about your new environment in a journal.

◆

*In peace I will lie down and sleep, for you alone,*
*Lord, make me dwell in safety.*
PSALM 4:8 NIV

◆

Spruce up your new home and make it reflect your personality. Buy a rug, frame some favorite photos and hang them on the walls, or hit some yard sales to find furniture you can refinish. Do some things to make the space your own. This will make it feel more like home.

# The Job Hunt: Finding My Place

Unable to get any internships, I worked a lot of really terrible summer jobs throughout college. I sold fireworks, painted semitrucks, cleaned hotel rooms, walked dogs, and scrubbed swimming pools. By my junior year, I felt doomed. Who was going to hire someone like me with no professional experience whatsoever? That's when I turned to online freelance work. I found dozens of sites that offered great opportunities to graphic/web designers, writers, computer programmers, marketing gurus, and translators. And the best part was that once I had built up a reliable reputation, freelance employers started seeking me out. Not only was I gaining valuable résumé experience, but I could choose what kind of work I wanted to do and how much I'd get paid for it. If only I had known about freelance opportunities sooner!

ASHLEY CASTEEL, 23

Some people grow up knowing exactly what they want to do in life. They are "born teachers," or they follow in a parent's footsteps to become a physician or a builder. Some begin working for a family business. Others are less certain of what they want to do. It can be a challenge to determine a career path, find a job, and begin working.

If you are looking for a job, take a deep breath. Remember that you are God's child, created with unique talents and abilities. The first step is to ask God to lead you.

God wants to be part of your everyday life. Pray throughout the day as you are seeking employment that the Lord will open and close doors to place you in the right position.

If you are unsure of what you want to do, there are interest and career questionnaires on the Internet that may be helpful. Most universities have a career guidance department. Perhaps you have studied to prepare for a certain type of work. Regardless, you need to prepare a résumé. There are various computer programs that will take you through a step-by-step process to design a professional résumé. Include all schooling, training, and work experience (paid and volunteer) that relates to the position for which you are applying.

Search for openings online, in the newspaper, and in career placement centers. Check every day as new job postings are added regularly. Consider sending an e-mail to friends and family and let them know about your job search. You might want to attach your résumé. Networking is a great way to find a job.

If you are called for an interview, do some research in order to learn about the organization. There are several books on the market that give tips for interview preparation. It is important to be on time, or even a little bit early. It is always better to be overdressed than underdressed when making a first impression. Smile, be confident, and try to relax. Most employers will ask if you have questions at the close of the interview. Feel free to ask questions. You are learning about the company and the position just as the employer is learning about you.

When you do land a job, go out to dinner with a friend or family member and celebrate! Remember to thank God for His provision of a job for you, and if you are not already tithing, this is a great time to begin giving 10 percent of your income to kingdom work through your church.

◆

*Lord, I am new at this. Please work behind the scenes as I do my part by actively looking. I want to honor You in my work. Provide the job that You know will be the best fit for me, I pray. Amen.*

*If any of you lacks wisdom, you should ask God, who gives generously to all without finding fault, and it will be given to you.*

JAMES 1:5 NIV

◆

Remember that you are informing the prospective employer about your qualifications. It is not bragging when you confidently state the characteristics you possess that would make you a great employee.

◆

*I instruct you in the way of wisdom and lead you along straight paths.*

PROVERBS 4:11 NIV

◆

Invest in an interview outfit appropriate for the jobs you are applying for. This will help you to avoid the stress of finding something to wear to an interview if you are invited to one without much time to prepare.

◆

*Wait for the LORD; be strong and take heart and wait for the LORD.*

PSALM 27:14 NIV

Pray for God to open and close doors for you throughout your job search. Then, trust Him when He does.

◆

*What is mankind that you are mindful of them, human beings that you care for them? You have made them a little lower than the angels and crowned them with glory and honor. You made them rulers over the works of your hands; you put everything under their feet.*

PSALM 8:4–6 NIV

◆

*There are different kinds of spiritual gifts, but the same Spirit is the source of them all. There are different kinds of service, but we serve the same Lord. God works in different ways, but it is the same God who does the work in all of us.*

1 CORINTHIANS 12:4–6 NLT

◆

Discover what you love, chase your dream, and know that even when you may have forgotten God, He hasn't forgotten you. He has provided guidance, love, and talent to you. Use those gifts to their highest ability, and know that He is there to show you the way when you've strayed from the path.

NICOLE RENEE HALE, 21

*Trust in the LORD with all your heart and lean not on your own understanding; in all your ways submit to him, and he will make your paths straight.*

PROVERBS 3:5–6 NIV

◆

Think about the types of questions that you may be asked at an interview. You may wish to purchase an interview guidebook. Ask a friend or family member to help you practice interviewing.

◆

*Those who know your name trust in you, for you, LORD, have never forsaken those who seek you.*

PSALM 9:10 NIV

◆

Unless you are 100 percent sure that you want to accept a position, it is a good idea to ask for at least twenty-four hours to think it over first. Take some time to think and pray about it rather than making a rash decision.

◆

*Do not be anxious about anything, but in every situation, by prayer and petition, with thanksgiving, present your requests to God.*

PHILIPPIANS 4:6 NIV

# Courage for Every Day

*"Be strong and courageous, and do the work.*
*Don't be afraid or discouraged, for the Lord God,*
*my God, is with you. He will not fail you or forsake you."*
1 CHRONICLES 28:20 NLT

For Theresa, it had been a long summer. Her grandmother passed away after a lengthy battle with cancer, and her relationship with her parents was strained. She was getting ready to start graduate school, and money was tight. With her future looming before her like a giant mountain, Theresa wasn't at all sure she had the strength to climb it.

Perhaps you know how Theresa feels. Whether it's job or money troubles, relationship difficulties, or just a bad day, it is all too easy to get discouraged by the size of the tasks that lie ahead.

David spoke the words in 1 Chronicles 28:20 to the Israelites, who were no doubt overwhelmed by *their* task, which was to build God's temple. David spoke the truth—God was with them, and with His help the Israelites successfully climbed that mountain.

Perhaps you're standing at the base of a giant mountain, looking at the rocks above and the steep climb ahead and wondering how on earth you're ever going to make it. Have courage! God promises to go before you and enable you to do things that seem beyond your abilities and strength.

So what are you waiting for? It's time to get your hiking shoes.

*But Jesus spoke to them at once. "Don't be afraid,"*
*he said. "Take courage. I am here!"*
MATTHEW 14:27 NLT

◆

*Wait on the LORD; be of good courage, and He shall*
*strengthen your heart; wait, I say, on the LORD!*
PSALM 27:14 NKJV

◆

*Be on guard. Stand firm in the faith.*
*Be courageous. Be strong.*
1 CORINTHIANS 16:13 NLT

◆

*So we say with confidence, "The Lord is my helper;*
*I will not be afraid. What can mere mortals do to me?"*
HEBREWS 13:6 NIV

◆

*For God has not given us a spirit of fear,*
*but of power and of love and of a sound mind.*
2 TIMOTHY 1:7 NKJV

◆

*In the fear of the LORD there is strong confidence,*
*and His children will have a place of refuge.*
PROVERBS 14:26 NKJV

*Be brave. Be strong. Don't give up.*
*Expect GOD to get here soon.*

PSALM 31:24 MSG

◆

*I can do all things through Christ who strengthens me.*

PHILIPPIANS 4:13 NKJV

◆

*For the LORD will be at your side and*
*will keep your foot from being snared.*

PROVERBS 3:26 NIV

◆

*So, friends, we can now—without hesitation—walk right up*
*to God, into "the Holy Place." Jesus has cleared the way by*
*the blood of his sacrifice, acting as our priest before God.*
*The "curtain" into God's presence is his body.*

HEBREWS 10:19-21 MSG

◆

*"Have I not commanded you? Be strong and of*
*good courage; do not be afraid, nor be dismayed,*
*for the LORD your God is with you wherever you go."*

JOSHUA 1:9 NKJV

*"Do not be afraid, little flock, for your Father
has been pleased to give you the kingdom."*

LUKE 12:32 NIV

◆

*"Be strong. Take courage. Don't be intimidated.
Don't give them a second thought because GOD,
your God, is striding ahead of you. He's right there
with you. He won't let you down; he won't leave you."*

DEUTERONOMY 31:6 MSG

◆

*"Fear nothing in the things you're about to suffer—
but stay on guard! Fear nothing! . . . Don't quit,
even if it costs you your life. Stay there believing.
I have a Life-Crown sized and ready for you."*

REVELATION 2:10 MSG

# Landing the Job: Work

If you can anticipate the next step, problem, solution, or opportunity, then you will stand out and earn the respect of your boss. Look one, two, and three steps down the road instead of staring at your feet and you will be a valuable asset to the company.

TANNER COPE, 20

So, you landed a job! Sometimes after a job search ends, it takes awhile to sink in that you won't be spending your time looking for work anymore. Instead, you will be working!

Did a schoolteacher ever remind you that school was your "job"? You learned early on that you had to show up to class on time—prepared—or else things did not go well for you. It's the same with your new job. There is a time you are to show up, duties you are to perform, and a level of professionalism and courtesy you should demonstrate on the job. Ephesians 6:7 (NLT) says to work "as though you were working for the Lord rather than for people." What does this mean to you? It means that regardless of your duties, you can do them for the glory of God.

Does your attitude bring God glory? Do you stand out in the workplace as a Christian, or do you save that for Sundays?

Sometimes it can be tempting to steal from your

employer. Oh, most of us are not tempted to steal monetarily, but consider these temptations: Are you tempted to leave early when the boss is not there? She'll never know. Do you send personal e-mails throughout the day and check Facebook regularly? This is robbing your employer of time for which you are being paid to work. Avoid this temptation. Work as though you are working for the Lord. Give your employer your very best.

Honesty is always the best policy. If something you are asked to do on the job seems "fishy" to you, it most likely is. As a believer, you have the Holy Spirit as your guide. The Spirit counsels you. If you sense that nagging feeling inside that something is unethical, take heed. It may be that God is providing a way out, a chance for you to choose to do right in a situation. You may not always get ahead by doing the right thing, but you will be at peace with who you are and how you conduct yourself. This is far more important than a promotion or a bigger paycheck.

Work as unto the Lord. Respect your employer. Have a good attitude. Do your best. Be honest. Let the Spirit lead you. These are guidelines to a successful work life. Enjoy your new job!

*God, thank You for my job. Help me as*
*I seek to honor You in my work. Amen.*

Change is inevitable. You will most likely have more
than one job in your adult life, multiple employers
or supervisors, and a variety of roles. You may change
offices, locations, or even cities. Embrace change
in your work. It keeps things fresh!

◆

*"Yes, always use honest weights and measures,*
*so that you may enjoy a long life in the land*
*the Lord your God is giving you."*
DEUTERONOMY 25:15 NLT

◆

Seek out other Christians in your workplace.
Organize a morning prayer time or Bible study.

◆

*"Observe the Sabbath day by keeping it holy, as the Lord*
*your God has commanded you. Six days you shall labor*
*and do all your work, but the seventh day is a sabbath*
*to the Lord your God. On it you shall not do any work."*
DEUTERONOMY 5:12–14 NIV

◆

Be on time. This honors your employer or your
employees. It honors those you work with and
those that you serve in your line of work.

Draw a line between your work life and your social life. Things can get complicated when your circle of friends is also your circle of colleagues.

◆

*Those who work their land will have abundant food, but those who chase fantasies will have their fill of poverty.*
PROVERBS 28:19 NIV

◆

Remember the common acronym from a few years back, WWJD? What would Jesus do? Always a good idea to keep this in mind in your work.

◆

*Through laziness, the rafters sag; because of idle hands, the house leaks.*
ECCLESIASTES 10:18 NIV

◆

Organization can help you to be more effective in your job. Keep sticky notes handy. Write yourself reminders and put them in a prominent place. It is good to have a "to do" or "to deal with ASAP" bin or folder.

◆

*Work willingly at whatever you do, as though you were working for the Lord rather than for people.*
COLOSSIANS 3:23 NLT

*Commit to the LORD whatever you do,*
*and he will establish your plans.*
PROVERBS 16:3 NIV

◆

Your workplace is a mission field. Jesus said that the
"harvest is plentiful but the workers are few" (Matthew 9:37
NIV). Work for the kingdom of the Lord. Go into your
office, your classroom, or your company with a heart
and a boldness that points others to your Savior.

◆

*May the favor of the Lord our God rest on us; establish the*
*work of our hands for us—yes, establish the work of our hands.*
PSALM 90:17 NIV

◆

You will spend many hours working in your lifetime.
Choose your occupation wisely. Make it something
that fits your gifts and abilities well, something you
see as worthy of your time and effort.

◆

*The LORD God took the man and put him in the*
*Garden of Eden to work it and take care of it.*
GENESIS 2:15 NIV

# LITTLE THINGS BECOME BIG THINGS

*"His master replied, 'Well done, good and faithful servant! You have been faithful with a few things; I will put you in charge of many things. Come and share your master's happiness!'"*

MATTHEW 25:23 NIV

◆

When Megan saw a newspaper ad looking for a floral designer at an upscale flower shop, she was confident that it was the perfect job for her. She loved to design trendy and unique arrangements and had even sold some to a couple of her mom's friends. Unfortunately, the shop manager wouldn't hire her because she lacked formal training.

Megan faced a reality that is common to many new grads. "We'd love to hire you, but you lack experience." But just how is a person supposed to get experience if no one ever hires her?

Jesus addresses this issue from a spiritual perspective when He tells the parable of the talents in Matthew 25. There He says that as we demonstrate trustworthiness with little things, God will gradually increase our responsibilities, entrusting us with bigger and more important tasks.

If you lack experience, there are many things you can do to show your trustworthiness. Take on small jobs in your field of interest. Look for places to volunteer your services. Pray for opportunities to showcase your talents. Those little efforts will be rewarded, and after a while they'll add up to a lifetime of worthwhile experience.

*Whatever your hand finds to do,*
*do it with your might.*
ECCLESIASTES 9:10 NKJV

*Even when we were with you, we gave you this rule:*
*"The one who is unwilling to work shall not eat."*
2 THESSALONIANS 3:10 NIV

*Hard work always pays off;*
*mere talk puts no bread on the table.*
PROVERBS 14:23 MSG

*"It is [the Lord your God] who blesses you with bountiful*
*harvests and gives you success in all your work.*
*This festival will be a time of great joy for all."*
DEUTERONOMY 16:15 NLT

*"But you, be strong and do not let your hands be weak,*
*for your work shall be rewarded!"*
2 CHRONICLES 15:7 NKJV

*You worked hard and deserve all you've got coming.*
*Enjoy the blessing! Revel in the goodness!*
PSALM 128:2 MSG

*So, my dear brothers and sisters, be strong and immovable.
Always work enthusiastically for the Lord, for you know that
nothing you do for the Lord is ever useless.*

1 CORINTHIANS 15:58 NLT

◆

*Don't be too fond of sleep; you'll end up in the poorhouse.
Wake up and get up; then there'll be food on the table.*

PROVERBS 20:13 MSG

◆

*"You have six days each week for your ordinary work,
but the seventh day is a Sabbath day of rest
dedicated to the LORD your God."*

EXODUS 20:9–10 NLT

◆

*Those who work their land will have abundant food,
but those who chase fantasies have no sense.*

PROVERBS 12:11 NIV

◆

*If you are a thief, quit stealing. Instead, use your hands for
good hard work, and then give generously to others in need.*

EPHESIANS 4:28 NLT

◆

*Now he who plants and he who waters are one, and each one
will receive his own reward according to his own labor.*

1 CORINTHIANS 3:8 NKJV

# Getting It Done: Time Management

It is extremely important to have balance in one's life, especially when adjusting to new circumstances and surroundings. Making time for a quiet time with Jesus every day is essential to growing in Him and seeking His will. By making sure that I put God first, He helps me to prioritize every other area in my life.

EMILY HOERNSCHEMEYER, 20

There will always be just twenty-four hours in a day. No matter how much you accomplish (or don't!), rejoice or complain, those hours will come and go. They are given to you by God to live to the fullest. Each new day of life should be celebrated as a gift.

God wants us to work. He created the world in six days, and on the seventh He rested. God did not *need* to rest. He rested so we would have an example to follow. We are to work hard, but we are also to remember when it is time to rest. Life can become unbalanced quickly if we don't hone our time-management skills.

The work week begins with a bang. Monday morning never waits. It comes, like the finder in Hide and Seek, whether we are "ready or not!" Before you find yourself snowed under with piles of work to complete both at your job and at home, think about how you will manage your time.

Make a list. Compile all the things you need to accomplish during the coming week and organize your list in a way that works for you. Keep the list in a place where it will always be easily accessible like in your purse or wallet, on your desk, or even posted on a bulletin board or on your refrigerator. As you complete the tasks, check them off your list.

Keeping a calendar is also helpful for time management. Whether it is a handheld device, a wall or desk calendar, or a daily planner, a calendar will remind you of upcoming events. As soon as you schedule a meeting, are assigned a due date, or make plans with a friend, record it on your calendar.

Besides lists and calendars, other time-management helps might include thinking through your weeknights. Is it reasonable to schedule something for every weeknight? Should you consider keeping two to three nights open each week so that you can take care of laundry or housekeeping and simply have some down time to spend alone? Our tendency is often to schedule our lives so heavily that by the weekend, we reach a point of exhaustion. Be cautious not to do this. Proper time management will even help you to stay healthy, especially if you remember to schedule time for regular exercise and enough sleep.

*Lord, teach me to manage my time in
a way that will honor You. Amen.*

*She watches over the affairs of her household*
*and does not eat the bread of idleness.*
PROVERBS 31:27 NIV

◆

If your home is getting messy throughout the week,
and the weekend is nowhere in sight, try setting a
kitchen timer for fifteen minutes and hold a speed-
cleaning session. You will be amazed how much tidier
your place will be after just a few minutes!

◆

Think ahead. Buy a booklet of stamps when you are at the
post office to mail a package. While grocery shopping,
double up on the items you tend to run out of quickly.
This will save you some extra trips!

◆

Remember that it is important to take time for your meals
and for exercise. You will feel better and be more alert if you
do not attempt to work around the clock. Your production at
work will actually increase if you take care of yourself.

◆

Try heading for bed fifteen minutes earlier than you
normally do. Resist hitting the SNOOZE button
more than one time each morning.

*There is a time for everything, and a season
for every activity under the heavens.*
ECCLESIASTES 3:1 NIV

◆

Set up an online bill payment program. Have insurance
or other monthly payments automatically withdrawn from
your bank account. Withdraw a certain amount of cash
each weekend to carry you through the coming week.
All of these are wise tips that will help you save time
and keep you from worrying about money.

◆

*So then, let us not be like others, who are asleep,
but let us be awake and sober.*
1 THESSALONIANS 5:6 NIV

◆

Start each day with prayer. Ask God to help you manage
your time. When you find yourself stressed about time,
ask Him to multiply your time for you. He wants to
be involved in the details of your life.

◆

Be a multi-tasker. Read while you walk on the treadmill.
Make a grocery list while you wait for your car to get an oil
change. Multi-tasking is a great time-management tool.

# The Blessing of Spiritual Discipline

*In the morning, L<small>ORD</small>, you hear my voice; in the morning*
*I lay my requests before you and wait expectantly.*
<small>PSALM 5:3 NIV</small>

**N**o team takes the field without first meeting in the locker room for a pregame talk. No actor takes the stage without first getting into character. It would be foolish to build a house without consulting with an architect and drawing up plans. Adequate preparation is the first essential step for any successful endeavor.

Throughout His earthly ministry, Jesus modeled this principle. He was an incredibly busy man. There were disciples to train, people to heal, and children to bless. No matter what He did or where He traveled, something or someone seemed to always need attention. But despite the many demands placed on Him, scripture tells us that Jesus got up early in the morning to take time to meet His Father in prayer.

What is the first thing you do each morning? Many of us hit the ground running, armed with to do lists a mile long. Unfortunately, this means that we often lack focus and fall into bed at night wondering if we really accomplished anything at all. While it doesn't ensure perfection, setting aside even a short time each morning to focus on the Father can help prepare us to live for Him.

How will you start your day today?

*Then Jehoshaphat added, "But first
let's find out what the LORD says."*
1 KINGS 22:5 NLT

◆

*You will guide me with Your counsel.*
PSALM 73:24 NKJV

◆

*Very early in the morning, while it was still dark,
Jesus got up, left the house and went off to
a solitary place, where he prayed.*
MARK 1:35 NIV

◆

*I will instruct you and teach
you in the way you should go.*
PSALM 32:8 NKJV

◆

*I rise before the dawning of the morning,
and cry for help; I hope in Your word.*
PSALM 119:147 NKJV

◆

*Strong God, I'm watching you do it, I can always
count on you—God, my dependable love.*
PSALM 59:17 MSG

*Satisfy us in the morning with your unfailing love,*
*that we may sing for joy and be glad all our days.*
PSALM 90:14 NIV

◆

*O LORD, be gracious to us; we have waited for You. Be their*
*arm every morning, our salvation also in the time of trouble.*
ISAIAH 33:2 NKJV

◆

*Let the morning bring me word of your unfailing love,*
*for I have put my trust in you. Show me the way*
*I should go, for to you I entrust my life.*
PSALM 143:8 NIV

◆

*GOD's loyal love couldn't have run out, his merciful*
*love couldn't have dried up. They're created new*
*every morning. How great your faithfulness!*
LAMENTATIONS 3:22–23 MSG

◆

*Lead me by your truth and teach me, for you are the*
*God who saves me. All day long I put my hope in you.*
PSALM 25:5 NLT

# Don't Give Up: Developing Perseverance

My father still keeps a suitcase filled with the (literally)
hundreds of rejection letters he received when he was job
hunting after he graduated college. He showed it to me my
junior year when we were cleaning up the basement, and
needless to say, it discouraged me. Sure, he had eventually
been offered a job (the same one he's had for twenty years),
but I was worried that I wouldn't be able to handle that kind
of rejection. I prayed about the situation, and God helped
me build up my courage and patience. And when I did
finally get a job, I understood why my father had held on
to all those rejection letters for so many years: to remind
himself that perseverance always pays off in the end.

ASHLEY CASTEEL, 23

"Stick-to-it-iveness" is a trait possessed by many who have
made a mark on the world. The ability to stand strong
through trials and temporary setbacks is a must if we're going
to find success in any area of life. The Bible tells us that we can
do all things through Christ's strength (see Philippians 4:13).

As you face hard times in your studies, your career
path, or your personal life, remember that growth is often
the result of trials. No one *wants* to go through trials. If only
every day could be our best day! If only every attempt could
end in a victory! But instead, sometimes hurdles, failures,
and delays in gratification will come your way.

Have you ever spent time with an elderly Christian whom you respect? He or she undoubtedly has a life story dotted with both highs and lows. While walking through the struggles is not pleasant, God is in the business of working all things together for good. It is a promise in Romans 8:28.

James 1:2–4 (NIV) says it this way: "Consider it pure joy, my brothers and sisters, whenever you face trials of many kinds, because you know that the testing of your faith produces perseverance. Let perseverance finish its work so that you may be mature and complete, not lacking anything."

The two words *mature* and *complete* are linked together here. Completeness does not come without maturity, and maturity is the result of perseverance.

Trust the Lord to see you through tough times. Considering trials as "pure joy" may seem like a crazy demand, but think about the reasoning behind such a statement. God sees our lives from a completely different perspective than we see them. We sit at the table looking at all the pieces, turning them over and examining them to try to imagine how they could fit together. He sees the pieces as a completed jigsaw puzzle, a beautiful picture. God knows that in order for the picture of our life to be complete, we must grow through trials.

Perseverance. Maturity. Wholeness in Christ. Be a man or woman whose life is marked by "stick-to-it-iveness." God is not finished with you yet!

*Develop in me a strength of character
that will bring You glory. Amen.*

*For this very reason, make every effort to add to your faith goodness; and to goodness, knowledge; and to knowledge, self-control; and to self-control, perseverance; and to perseverance, godliness; and to godliness, mutual affection; and to mutual affection, love.*

2 PETER 1:5-7 NIV

◆

*Watch, stand fast in the faith, be brave, be strong. Let all that you do be done with love.*

1 CORINTHIANS 16:13-14 NKJV

◆

*And we boast in the hope of the glory of God. Not only so, but we also glory in our sufferings, because we know that suffering produces perseverance; perseverance, character; and character, hope.*

ROMANS 5:2-4 NIV

◆

*We have confidence in the Lord that you are doing and will continue to do the things we command. May the Lord direct your hearts into God's love and Christ's perseverance.*

2 THESSALONIANS 3:4-5 NIV

*Blessed is the one who perseveres under trial because,*
*having stood the test, that person will receive the crown*
*of life that the Lord has promised to those who love him.*
JAMES 1:12 NIV

*By faith he [Moses] left Egypt, not fearing the king's anger;*
*he persevered because he saw him who is invisible.*
HEBREWS 11:27 NIV

*Watch your life and doctrine closely.*
*Persevere in them, because if you do,*
*you will save both yourself and your hearers.*
1 TIMOTHY 4:16 NIV

*Brothers and sisters, as an example of patience in the*
*face of suffering, take the prophets who spoke in the name*
*of the Lord. As you know, we count as blessed those who*
*have persevered. You have heard of Job's perseverance*
*and have seen what the Lord finally brought about.*
*The Lord is full of compassion and mercy.*
JAMES 5:10–11 NIV

# THE WAITING GAME

*The LORD kept his word and did for Sarah exactly*
*what he had promised. She became pregnant,*
*and she gave birth to a son for Abraham in his old age.*
*This happened at just the time God had said it would.*

In Genesis 15 God told Abraham—an old and childless man—that he would have so many descendants he would never be able to count them all.

Instead of waiting on God, Abraham's wife, Sarah, decided to take matters into her own hands by offering her maidservant, Hagar, to Abraham. This relationship resulted in the birth of Ishmael. You can imagine the problems this caused between the two women.

Later, when she was blessed with her own son, Isaac, Sarah must have wondered why she didn't simply wait for God's plan to be fulfilled. His plan was *so* much better than hers.

Have you ever prayed for something, then told God how to make it happen? The problem is that when we take matters into our own hands, we're limiting God's work in our lives. What are you waiting for today? Are you waiting to hear about a job offer or acceptance to the school of your choice? Wondering if your long-term relationship will turn into marriage? Whatever your need, give it to God. Relax and let Him handle it for you. The results will be better than you could ever dream.

*This calls for patient endurance on the part of the people of God who keep his commands and remain faithful to Jesus.*

REVELATION 14:12 NIV

◆

*Let us hold fast the confession of our hope without wavering, for He who promised is faithful.*

HEBREWS 10:23 NKJV

◆

*Now may the Lord direct your hearts into the love of God and into the patience of Christ.*

2 THESSALONIANS 3:5 NKJV

◆

*So let's not allow ourselves to get fatigued doing good. At the right time we will harvest a good crop if we don't give up, or quit.*

GALATIANS 6:9 MSG

◆

*To him who overcomes I will grant to sit with Me on My throne, as I also overcame and sat down with My Father on His throne.*

REVELATION 3:21 NKJV

◆

*For you have need of endurance, so that after you have done the will of God, you may receive the promise.*

HEBREWS 10:36 NKJV

*I have fought the good fight, I have finished the race,
I have kept the faith. Now there is in store for me the crown
of righteousness, which the Lord, the righteous Judge,
will award to me on that day—and not only to me,
but also to all who have longed for his appearing.*

2 TIMOTHY 4:7–8 NIV

*Therefore put on the full armor of God, so that when the day
of evil comes, you may be able to stand your ground,
and after you have done everything, to stand.*

EPHESIANS 6:13 NIV

*Everyone who competes in the games goes into strict
training. They do it to get a crown that will not last,
but we do it to get a crown that will last forever.*

1 CORINTHIANS 9:25 NIV

*He will give eternal life to those who keep
on doing good, seeking after the glory and
honor and immortality that God offers.*

ROMANS 2:7 NLT

# My Priorities

*When Jesus heard this, he said to him, "You still lack one thing. Sell everything you have and give to the poor, and you will have treasure in heaven. Then come, follow me."*

LUKE 18:22 NIV

When the rich young ruler approached Jesus, he was sure he'd covered all the bases. The young man knew the law and had followed it to the letter since he was a boy. However, Jesus threw him a curveball. "All this stuff you love," Jesus said, "get rid of it. Then follow Me." Jesus' candid answer made the young man very sad because he had a lot of stuff he loved. He'd arrived. He was, perhaps, at the pinnacle of his career. Who was Jesus to ask him to give it all away?

Scripture tells us that anything we put in place of Christ on His throne in our lives is idolatry. We, as humans, are easily distracted—by wealth, material success, fame. . .the things we often envy in others when we don't possess them ourselves. The truth is, in the light of eternity, these things are worthless.

Is there anything in your life that is taking the place of Jesus? What is He asking you to give up? The cost of following Him is high, but the rewards are eternal and far too incredible for words.

*"But don't be so concerned about perishable things like food. Spend your energy seeking the eternal life that the Son of Man can give you. For God the Father has given me the seal of his approval."*

JOHN 6:27 NLT

◆

*Now we live with great expectation, and we have a priceless inheritance—an inheritance that is kept in heaven for you, pure and undefiled, beyond the reach of change and decay.*

1 PETER 1:3-4 NLT

◆

*"For God so loved the world that He gave His only begotten Son, that whoever believes in Him should not perish but have everlasting life."*

JOHN 3:16 NKJV

◆

*This truth gives them confidence that they have eternal life, which God—who does not lie— promised them before the world began.*

TITUS 1:2 NLT

◆

*"For where your treasure is, there your heart will be also."*

LUKE 12:34 NKJV

*He has given us eternal life, and this life is in his Son. Whoever has the Son has life; whoever does not have God's Son does not have life. I have written this to you who believe in the name of the Son of God, so that you may know you have eternal life.*

1 John 5:11–13 NLT

*"The kingdom of heaven is like treasure hidden in a field, which a man found and hid; and for joy over it he goes and sells all that he has and buys that field."*

Matthew 13:44 NKJV

*In this way they will lay up treasure for themselves as a firm foundation for the coming age, so that they may take hold of the life that is truly life.*

1 Timothy 6:19 NIV

*Work hard for sin your whole life and your pension is death. But God's gift is real life, eternal life, delivered by Jesus, our Master.*

Romans 6:23 MSG

*"The righteous will go into eternal life."*
MATTHEW 25:46 NLT

◆

*"The water I give will be an artesian spring within,
gushing fountains of endless life."*
JOHN 4:14 MSG

◆

*Make no mistake: In the end you get what's coming
to you—Real Life for those who work on God's side.*
ROMANS 2:7 MSG

◆

*And when the Chief Shepherd appears, you will
receive the crown of glory that will never fade away.*
1 PETER 5:4 NIV

◆

*So that, having been justified by his grace, we might
become heirs having the hope of eternal life.*
TITUS 3:7 NIV

◆

*"Now this is eternal life: that they may know you,
the only true God, and Jesus Christ, whom you have sent."*
JOHN 17:3 NIV

# Missing the Mark: Failure

*So now there is no condemnation*
*for those who belong to Christ Jesus.*
ROMANS 8:1 NLT

◆

J ustin wished for a time machine. He would give anything to turn back the clock a mere twelve hours.
What seemed like harmless fun last night left a terrible
aftertaste in Justin's mouth this morning—both literally
and figuratively. What was he thinking? And his fraternity
brothers knew he was a Christian, too. What kind of a
witness had he been? Ugh. What a mess. Justin spent the
rest of the day beating himself up. How would he ever
recover from such a failure?

One of the consequences of sin is feeling guilt and
shame for our actions. On one hand, guilt serves an
important purpose—it forces us to come to grips with the
condition of our hearts. But after that, guilt should point us
to Christ so that we can ask for and receive the forgiveness
that is promised to us.

The problem is, many of us get stuck in our guilt. We
begin to feel worthless instead of unworthy, condemned
instead of forgiven. But this is not the truth that Jesus
offers. There is no unforgivable sin and no action that God
cannot redeem. Move past the sin in your life to a place of
healing and forgiveness. It's a gift God has promised to you
that you'll find right at the foot of the cross.

*Blessed is he whose transgression is forgiven,*
*whose sin is covered.*
PSALM 32:1 NKJV

◆

*"For I will forgive their wickedness and*
*will remember their sins no more."*
HEBREWS 8:12 NIV

◆

*"No longer will they teach their neighbor, or say to one another,*
*'Know the LORD,' because they will all know me, from the least*
*of them to the greatest," declares the LORD. "For I will forgive*
*their wickedness and will remember their sins no more."*
JEREMIAH 31:34 NIV

◆

*If we confess our sins, He is faithful and just to forgive*
*us our sins and to cleanse us from all unrighteousness.*
1 JOHN 1:9 NKJV

◆

*"Then if my people who are called by my name will humble*
*themselves and pray and seek my face and turn from*
*their wicked ways, I will hear from heaven and will*
*forgive their sins and restore their land."*
2 CHRONICLES 7:14 NLT

*"I'll scrub them clean from the dirt they've done against me.*
*I'll forgive everything they've done wrong,*
*forgive all their rebellions."*

JEREMIAH 33:8 MSG

*Bring your confessions, and return to the LORD.*
*Say to him, "Forgive all our sins and graciously receive us,*
*so that we may offer you our praises."*

HOSEA 14:2 NLT

*Seeing then that we have a great High Priest who has*
*passed through the heavens, Jesus the Son of God, let us*
*hold fast our confession. For we do not have a High Priest*
*who cannot sympathize with our weaknesses, but was in*
*all points tempted as we are, yet without sin.*

HEBREWS 4:14–15 NKJV

*Who then will condemn us? No one—for Christ Jesus died*
*for us and was raised to life for us, and he is sitting in the*
*place of honor at God's right hand, pleading for us.*

ROMANS 8:34 NLT

*"Blessed are those who mourn,*
*for they will be comforted."*
MATTHEW 5:4 NIV

◆

*"For if you forgive men their trespasses,*
*your heavenly Father will also forgive you."*
MATTHEW 6:14 NKJV

◆

*And the result of God's gracious gift is very different*
*from the result of that one man's sin. For Adam's sin led to*
*condemnation, but God's free gift leads to our being made*
*right with God, even though we are guilty of many sins.*
ROMANS 5:16 NLT

◆

*If the ministry that brought condemnation was glorious, how*
*much more glorious is the ministry that brings righteousness!*
2 CORINTHIANS 3:9 NIV

◆

*This is how we know that we belong to the truth and*
*how we set our hearts at rest in his presence: If our*
*hearts condemn us, we know that God is greater*
*than our hearts, and he knows everything.*
1 JOHN 3:19-20 NIV

# Tough Times

*Neither height nor depth, nor anything else in
all creation, will be able to separate us from the
love of God that is in Christ Jesus our Lord.*

ROMANS 8:39 NIV

John hung up the phone, grateful his roommate was out for the evening. His dad just dropped a bombshell—how could his parents be divorcing after all these years? If they couldn't make it, how could anyone? Throughout the night, John wrestled with his feelings and cried out to God. He felt as if the very foundation of his world had been shattered. *What am I supposed to do now?* he wondered.

Has the foundation of your world ever been shattered? Perhaps, like John, you've received news that your parents are splitting up. That you didn't pass an important exam. That someone you thought was a friend turned out to be an enemy. Life can deal some pretty harsh blows sometimes.

Situations like these can cause us to question God's love. Why would a loving God let us suffer in this way? Unfortunately, there are no easy answers. However, we can rest on one solid truth—God is in control. He loves you. Nothing can change that. Your world could be caving in right now, but there is nothing that can ever separate you from God's love. Rest in Him.

*The Lord is good, a stronghold in the day of trouble;*
*and He knows those who trust in Him.*

NAHUM 1:7 NKJV

◆

*These hard times are small potatoes compared to the*
*coming good times, the lavish celebration prepared for us.*
*There's far more here than meets the eye. The things we*
*see now are here today, gone tomorrow. But the*
*things we can't see now will last forever.*

2 CORINTHIANS 4:17–18 MSG

◆

*What then shall we say to these things?*
*If God is for us, who can be against us?*

ROMANS 8:31 NKJV

◆

*That is why we never give up. Though our bodies are dying,*
*our spirits are being renewed every day.*

2 CORINTHIANS 4:16 NLT

◆

*"Have I not commanded you? Be strong and of good*
*courage; do not be afraid, nor be dismayed, for the*
*Lord your God is with you wherever you go."*

JOSHUA 1:9 NKJV

*Because of the Lord's great love we are not consumed,
for his compassions never fail. They are new
every morning; great is your faithfulness.*

LAMENTATIONS 3:22–23 NIV

❖

*He gives power to the weak and strength to the powerless.*

ISAIAH 40:29 NLT

❖

*No one who hopes in you will ever be put to shame.*

PSALM 25:3 NIV

❖

*"When you go through deep waters, I will be with you.
When you go through rivers of difficulty, you will not
drown. When you walk through the fire of oppression,
you will not be burned up; the flames will not consume you."*

ISAIAH 43:2 NLT

❖

*Why, my soul, are you downcast? Why so disturbed
within me? Put your hope in God, for I will yet
praise him, my Savior and my God.*

PSALM 42:11 NIV

❖

*Give all your worries and cares to God,
for he cares about you.*

1 PETER 5:7 NLT

*You will keep him in perfect peace, whose mind
is stayed on You, because he trusts in You.*

ISAIAH 26:3 NKJV

◆

*Let all that I am wait quietly before God,
for my hope is in him.*

PSALM 62:5 NLT

◆

*Praise be to the God. . .who comforts us in all our troubles,
so that we can comfort those in any trouble with the
comfort we ourselves receive from God. For just as
we share abundantly in the sufferings of Christ,
so also our comfort abounds through Christ.*

2 CORINTHIANS 1:3–5 NIV

◆

*May integrity and honesty protect me,
for I put my hope in you.*

PSALM 25:21 NLT

◆

*Yet what we suffer now is nothing compared
to the glory he will reveal to us later.*

ROMANS 8:18 NLT

# One Truth

Todd loved baseball and really hoped to play in high school, but his eighth-grade gym teacher talked him out of it. "Give it up now, Todd—you definitely don't have what it takes to make the team." Todd got the message loud and clear. He went through all four years of high school never bothering to try out. Imagine his surprise when he became the star player on his intramural softball team in college.

Have you ever believed a lie about yourself? Moses did. In Exodus, when God called him to lead the children of Israel, Moses responded that he was "slow of speech." He doubted that people would listen to him (see Exodus 3–4). However, a different portrait of Moses is painted in the book of Acts. In Stephen's speech to the Sanhedrin, he says that Moses was "powerful in speech and action" (see Acts 7:20–36).

Many of us struggle to believe the truth about ourselves, just like Moses did. The lies we believe can come from many places, but ultimately, they come from Satan himself. What lies do you believe about yourself? How might those lies be preventing you from experiencing God's plan for *your* life?

*Lead me in Your truth and teach me, for You are
the God of my salvation; on You I wait all the day.*

PSALM 25:5 NKJV

◆

*Jesus answered, "I am the way and the truth and the life.
No one comes to the Father except through me."*

JOHN 14:6 NIV

◆

*Truth shall spring out of the earth,
and righteousness shall look down from heaven.*

PSALM 85:11 NKJV

◆

*He will wear righteousness like a belt
and truth like an undergarment.*

ISAIAH 11:5 NLT

◆

*Truth lasts; lies are here today, gone tomorrow.*

PROVERBS 12:19 MSG

◆

*We are from God, and whoever knows God listens to us; but
whoever is not from God does not listen to us. This is how we
recognize the Spirit of truth and the spirit of falsehood.*

1 JOHN 4:6 NIV

*But for those who are self-seeking and who reject the
truth and follow evil, there will be wrath and anger.*

ROMANS 2:8 NIV

◆

*I have chosen the way of truth;
Your judgments I have laid before me.*

PSALM 119:30 NKJV

◆

*"And you shall know the truth,
and the truth shall make you free."*

JOHN 8:32 NKJV

◆

*They exchanged the truth about God for a lie, and worshiped
and served created things rather than the Creator—
who is forever praised. Amen.*

ROMANS 1:25 NIV

◆

*"When the Spirit of truth comes, he will guide you into all
truth. He will not speak on his own but will tell you what
he has heard. He will tell you about the future."*

JOHN 16:13 NLT

◆

*Make them holy—consecrated—with the truth;
your word is consecrating truth.*

JOHN 17:17 MSG

# Wisdom for Life

*My son, if you accept my words and store up my commands within you...then you will understand the fear of the LORD and find the knowledge of God.*

PROVERBS 2:1, 5 NIV

E ven though we have many different types of electronic communication at our fingertips, it's still fun to receive a letter in the mail. Letters are especially sweet when they come from someone who loves us.

King Solomon wrote a wonderful letter to his sons in the Bible—better known as the book of Proverbs. At its core, this little gem is a heartfelt love letter from a father to his children—not only from Solomon to his sons, but from God to us.

Proverbs contains an abundance of short sayings that are as relevant to us now as they surely were to Solomon's sons centuries ago. The wisdom of Proverbs can apply to every area of our lives. It addresses everything from relationships to our finances and to our work habits.

*The righteous choose their friends carefully* (Proverbs 12:26 NIV).

*The greedy bring ruin to their households* (Proverbs 15:27 NIV).

*Commit to the LORD whatever you do, and he will establish your plans* (Proverbs 16:3 NIV).

These nuggets in scripture are timeless truths, guidelines for living, ways to increase your chances of success in life. Biblical success—righteousness, integrity, honesty, wisdom—that's yours for a lifetime.

*A wise youth harvests in the summer,*
*but one who sleeps during harvest is a disgrace.*
PROVERBS 10:5 NLT

◆

*Who is wise? Let him understand these things.*
*Who is prudent? Let him know them. For the ways*
*of the LORD are right; the righteous walk in them,*
*but transgressors stumble in them.*
HOSEA 14:9 NKJV

◆

*The way of a fool is right in his own eyes,*
*but he who heeds counsel is wise.*
PROVERBS 12:15 NKJV

◆

*Prudent people don't flaunt their knowledge;*
*talkative fools broadcast their silliness.*
PROVERBS 12:23 MSG

◆

*Lazy people want much but get little,*
*but those who work hard will prosper.*
PROVERBS 13:4 NLT

◆

*Plans fail for lack of counsel,*
*but with many advisers they succeed.*
PROVERBS 15:22 NIV

*The teaching of the wise is a fountain of life,*
*turning a person from the snares of death.*
PROVERBS 13:14 NIV

◆

*Even fools are thought wise when they keep silent;*
*with their mouths shut, they seem intelligent.*
PROVERBS 17:28 NLT

◆

*"Men and women who have lived wisely and well will*
*shine brilliantly, like the cloudless, star-strewn night*
*skies. And those who put others on the right path*
*to life will glow like stars forever."*
DANIEL 12:3 MSG

◆

*Why should fools have money in hand to buy wisdom,*
*when they are not able to understand it?*
PROVERBS 17:16 NIV

◆

*We humans keep brainstorming options and plans,*
*but GOD's purpose prevails.*
PROVERBS 19:21 MSG

◆

*He who follows righteousness and mercy finds life,*
*righteousness, and honor.*
PROVERBS 21:21 NKJV

# Choose Obedience

*Here now is my final conclusion: Fear God and*
*obey his commands, for this is everyone's duty.*
ECCLESIASTES 12:13 NLT

The plan was simple, and from Joe's perspective, extremely economical. The term paper was due the week after spring break. Joe wanted to go skiing, so he decided to hire someone to write the paper for him.

He tried to talk Mike into doing the same. "There's no way you can go skiing and get the term paper done, so do it my way and you can have the best of both worlds." There was only one problem. Joe's plan was wrong, and Mike knew it. In the end he decided to skip the ski trip and write his own paper. As far as he knew, Joe never got caught, but Mike was glad he could turn the paper in with a clear conscience, even if it did mean missing a week of skiing.

Choosing obedience sometimes means making a hard choice. Sometimes it's merely the sacrifice of convenience or comfort, but often the stakes are higher. Paul was obedient and it landed him in prison. Philippians 2 tells us that Jesus was obedient—to the point of death. You may not always be immediately rewarded for your obedience. But when you make choices that honor God, you can be sure that even if no one else notices, He is nodding His head with loving approval.

*"If you keep My commandments, you will abide
in My love, just as I have kept My Father's
commandments and abide in His love."*

JOHN 15:10 NKJV

◆

*Whatever you have learned or received or heard
from me, or seen in me—put it into practice.
And the God of peace will be with you.*

PHILIPPIANS 4:9 NIV

◆

*"What is more pleasing to the LORD: your burnt offerings
and sacrifices or your obedience to his voice?
Listen! Obedience is better than sacrifice."*

1 SAMUEL 15:22 NLT

◆

*"If they obey and serve him, they'll have a good, long life on
easy street. But if they disobey, they'll be cut down in
their prime and never know the first thing about life."*

JOB 36:11–12 MSG

◆

*For the person who keeps all of the laws except one is as
guilty as a person who has broken all of God's laws.*

JAMES 2:10 NLT

*"Knowing the correct password—saying 'Master, Master,' for instance—isn't going to get you anywhere with me. What is required is serious obedience— doing what my Father wills."*

MATTHEW 7:21 MSG

❖

*Obey your spiritual leaders, and do what they say. Their work is to watch over your souls, and they are accountable to God. Give them reason to do this with joy and not with sorrow. That would certainly not be for your benefit.*

HEBREWS 13:17 NLT

❖

*The LORD leads with unfailing love and faithfulness all who keep his covenant and obey his demands.*

PSALM 25:10 NLT

❖

*We know that we have come to know him if we keep his commands. . . . But if anyone obeys his word, love for God is truly made complete in them. This is how we know we are in him: Whoever claims to live in him must live as Jesus did.*

1 JOHN 2:3, 5-6 NIV

*"Oh, that they had such a heart in them that they would fear Me and always keep all My commandments, that it might be well with them and with their children forever!"*

DEUTERONOMY 5:29 NKJV

◆

*My son, do not forget my law, but let your heart keep my commands; for length of days and long life and peace they will add to you.*

PROVERBS 3:1–2 NKJV

◆

*Merely hearing God's law is a waste of your time if you don't do what he commands. Doing, not hearing, is what makes the difference with God.*

ROMANS 2:13 MSG

◆

*"Blessed rather are those who hear the word of God and obey it."*

LUKE 11:28 NIV

◆

*For I command you today to love the LORD your God, to walk in obedience to him, and to keep his commands, decrees and laws; then you will live and increase, and the LORD your God will bless you in the land you are entering to possess.*

DEUTERONOMY 30:16 NIV

# Thicker Than Water: My Family

My family is my physical support system. They are
always there to encourage me and offer me wisdom and
insight. I not only trust them, but I also enjoy spending
time with them and have established deep spiritual and
emotional relationships with each member.

EMILY HOERNSCHEMEYER, 20

---

Have you ever looked at someone else's family and
thought to yourself, *Why can't my family be that close?
That "normal"? That kind? That together?* In reality, there is
no perfect family. Each has a unique blend of personalities,
strengths, and weaknesses. Your family is a gift, and what
you do with it is up to you.

God's Word emphasizes that we are to honor our
parents. What does honoring your parents look like? It
looks different now that you are a recent graduate than it
did when you were a child, and yet the command remains.
Honor your parents by respecting them. You may not
always agree with their advice, but at least listen to it. They
are God-given authorities in your life, and as you transition
into adulthood, their role shifts to that of supportive friends.

To honor them also means that you should represent
them well. Wherever you go and whatever you do, for as
long as you live, you will represent your earthly parents.
You are a reflection of them. Will your ways bring them joy

or disgrace? Consider this as you make choices. Bring your family honor.

Siblings also are a gift from God. The age and personality differences between siblings affect these unique relationships. If you and your siblings are close in age or of very different dispositions, you may have experienced sibling rivalry while growing up. Now that you are older, seek to find places in those relationships that may need healing. Ask God to help you have grace with your siblings, to accept them as different from you, and to love them for who God made them to be.

Life is full of changes. Friends come and go, but your family is forever. Be cautious with how you speak to your family. You may have every reason in the world to be angry with a family member, but you can choose to love instead. Ask God to soften your heart in areas where it is hard. Sometimes it is difficult to love those closest in our lives.

Recognize that you are not part of your family by accident. God ordained these people for you to walk and grow with, belong to, and care for on this earth. He planted you in the family where you find yourself. A family is a wonderful blessing from God. A family is forever. Choose to appreciate yours. Seek to honor God in your family relationships.

◆

*Father, thank You for my family. We are a bunch of imperfect people. Help us to love one another well. Amen.*

*Children's children are a crown to the aged,*
*and parents are the pride of their children.*
PROVERBS 17:6 NIV

◆

Make it a part of your schedule to call home to talk to family once a week. No matter how far away you are, communicating with people back home on a regular basis will keep you connected.

◆

*Not looking to your own interests but each of you to the*
*interests of the others.*
PHILIPPIANS 2:4 NIV

◆

I have never been smarter than when I've kept my mouth shut. "Sin is not ended by multiplying words, but the prudent hold their tongues." Put Proverbs 10:19 (NIV) into practice and you will be amazed at how many conflicts are averted and how many feelings you will *not* hurt.
TANNER COPE, 20

◆

*"Honor your father and your mother, that your days may be*
*long upon the land which the LORD your God is giving you."*
EXODUS 20:12 NKJV

Respect differences in personalities within your family members. People have different strengths, weaknesses, communication styles, and love languages.

◆

*Large crowds were traveling with Jesus, and turning to them he said: "If anyone comes to me and does not hate father and mother, wife and children, brothers and sisters— yes, even their own life—such a person cannot be my disciple. And whoever does not carry their cross and follow me cannot be my disciple."*

Luke 14:25-27 niv

◆

*"Which of you fathers, if your son asks for a fish, will give him a snake instead? Or if he asks for an egg, will give him a scorpion? If you then, though you are evil, know how to give good gifts to your children, how much more will your Father in heaven give the Holy Spirit to those who ask him!"*

Luke 11:11-13 niv

◆

*Be completely humble and gentle; be patient, bearing with one another in love.*

Ephesians 4:2 niv

# Well-Seasoned Conversation

*Let your conversation be always full of grace, seasoned
with salt, so that you may know how to answer everyone.*
COLOSSIANS 4:6 NIV

One of your coworkers wants to take a long lunch with his girlfriend. If the boss notices, he wonders if you will cover for him—saying something like he called to say his car broke down and he's running late?

What do you say? How about: *"If you think I'm going to lie for you, think again. There's no way I'm going to jeopardize my job for you."* Or how about this? *"Hey, Rick, I don't feel comfortable saying something that isn't true. Can I help you figure out how to get your project done so you can leave for an early dinner instead?"*

One response puts your coworker on the defensive. The other response is equally straightforward, but it opens the door for future conversations and gives you an opportunity to help instead of criticize.

Colossians says our words should be "full of grace...[as if they are] seasoned with salt." Throughout Jesus' earthly ministry, He seasoned His words with just the right amount of grace. He never concealed the truth, but when He spoke, He put the needs of his listeners first.

Grace. Like salt on our food, it improves the flavor of our words and prevents us from saying things we might regret later. How can you season your words with grace today?

*Do not let any unwholesome talk come out of your mouths,
but only what is helpful for building others up according to
their needs, that it may benefit those who listen.*

EPHESIANS 4:29 NIV

◆

*Too much talk leads to sin.
Be sensible and keep your mouth shut.*

PROVERBS 10:19 NLT

◆

*It only takes a spark, remember, to set off a forest fire.
A careless or wrongly placed word out
of your mouth can do that.*

JAMES 3:5-6 MSG

◆

*"You must give an account on judgment day for
every idle word you speak. The words you say
will either acquit you or condemn you."*

MATTHEW 12:36-37 NLT

◆

*A man has joy by the answer of his mouth,
and a word spoken in due season, how good it is!*

PROVERBS 15:23 NKJV

*A soft answer turns away wrath,*
*but a harsh word stirs up anger.*
PROVERBS 15:1 NKJV

◆

*"If you want to enjoy life and see many happy days, keep your*
*tongue from speaking evil and your lips from telling lies."*
1 PETER 3:10 NLT

◆

*You must also rid yourselves of all such things*
*as these: anger, rage, malice, slander,*
*and filthy language from your lips.*
COLOSSIANS 3:8 NIV

◆

*Those who guard their mouths and their*
*tongues keep themselves from calamity.*
PROVERBS 21:23 NIV

◆

*Do not speak evil of one another, brethren. He who speaks*
*evil of a brother and judges his brother, speaks evil of*
*the law and judges the law. But if you judge the law,*
*you are not a doer of the law but a judge.*
JAMES 4:11 NKJV

*Like a north wind that brings unexpected rain
is a sly tongue—which provokes a horrified look.*

PROVERBS 25:23 NIV

◆

*The words of a wise person are gracious.
The talk of a fool self-destructs.*

ECCLESIASTES 10:12 MSG

◆

*There is gold and a multitude of rubies,
but the lips of knowledge are a precious jewel.*

PROVERBS 20:15 NKJV

◆

*Though some tongues just love the taste of gossip,
those who follow Jesus have better uses for language
than that. Don't talk dirty or silly. That kind of talk
doesn't fit our style. Thanksgiving is our dialect.*

EPHESIANS 5:3-4 MSG

◆

*Do you see a man hasty in his words?
There is more hope for a fool than for him.*

PROVERBS 29:20 NKJV

# Who I Hang With: My Friendships

You will make friends! I promise! The first year of college
all freshmen are in the same boat. I loved freshman year
because it is a rare opportunity to "start over." Who you
were in high school does not have to be the person you
are in college. Be yourself! Try new things you normally
wouldn't. College is a unique season of life where you are
able to encounter so many different and unique individuals
with whom you'll share the next four to five years.

MOLLY WEISGARBER, 22

How do you choose your friends? Have you come to
understand that there are various types of friends,
different levels of friendship, and that just a few precious
friendships stand the test of time?

There are friends that you share an interest with
and enjoy spending time with because of what you
have in common. This may be a running buddy, a book
club member, a guy on your football team, a girl you
scrapbook with, or a classmate who shares your passion for
photography. This type of friendship may deepen as time
passes.

Other friends enter your life due to proximity, such
as neighbors in your hometown or in the college dorm.
Some friends you'll meet through work, church, or other
friends. Some you grew up with or have known a very long

time. Have you ever been asked how you came to know a particular friend and found it hard to recall exactly how you met? It just seems that person has always been a part of your life, doesn't it?

Everyone needs friends that fill different roles. If you told your deepest, darkest secret to every friend you have, it wouldn't stay a secret long. If you have found a friend that you can trust, a friend that sticks around through the bad times as well as the good, you are blessed. Appreciate that friend. Seek to be a good friend in return. It takes being a good friend in order to have good friends.

Jesus chose friends. He walked with twelve men known as His "disciples" during His ministry here on earth. He spoke into their lives, lived among them, ate meals with them, traveled with them, and taught them in more specific ways than He taught the masses. The calling was not an easy one for these friends of the Savior. They left houses, families, and occupations to follow Christ. They laid down their lives for His cause.

The Word of God instructs us that we are to be *in this world* but that as Christians, we are not *of this world*. Know the difference? Certainly, Jesus was a friend to the unlovely and the unlovable—and we should be, too. He taught, however, that we are to be "equally yoked" in our dealings with others. Our closest companions, business associates, and certainly those we would look to for counsel should be Christians. The worldview of an unbeliever is vastly different from that of a believer. Seek out friends who know and love Jesus, and you can be sure that they will have your best interest at heart.

Some friends are for a lifetime. Others are for a season.
Accept this fact. Hold on to the friends that are lifelong. . .
but appreciate those that God puts in your life simply
for a particular time. Both are valuable treasures.

◆

*Do not be yoked together with unbelievers. For what do*
*righteousness and wickedness have in common?*
*Or what fellowship can light have with darkness?*
2 CORINTHIANS 6:14 NIV

◆

It is much easier for a friend to pull you down than for you
to pull a friend up. Make wise choices in the company you
keep. Your closest friends should be followers of Christ.

◆

*He who walks with wise men will be wise,*
*but the companion of fools will be destroyed.*
PROVERBS 13:20 NKJV

◆

*Dear friends, since God so loved us,*
*we also ought to love one another.*
1 JOHN 4:11 NIV

*Not giving up meeting together, as some are in the
habit of doing, but encouraging one another—
and all the more as you see the Day approaching.*

HEBREWS 10:25 NIV

◆

*One who has unreliable friends soon comes to ruin,
but there is a friend who sticks closer than a brother.*

PROVERBS 18:24 NIV

◆

Don't be afraid of silence with friends. It is good to learn
to be comfortable in another's presence without noise.

◆

*As iron sharpens iron, so a man sharpens
the countenance of his friend.*

PROVERBS 27:17 NKJV

◆

*A friend loves at all times, and a brother
is born for a time of adversity.*

PROVERBS 17:17 NIV

◆

*Wounds from a friend can be trusted,
but an enemy multiplies kisses.*

PROVERBS 27:6 NIV

# SOMETIMES YOU NEED A HAND

*Aaron and Hur held his hands up—one on one side, one on the other—so that his hands remained steady till sunset.*

Exodus 17:12 NIV

◆

It was a simple job. As long as he stood on a hill and held up his hands, the Israelites would have the upper hand in their battle with the Amalekites. If Moses lowered his hands, the Amalekites would take the lead. Despite the simplicity of his task, Moses soon learned he needed help.

That's where his friends Aaron and Hur came in. They put a rock under Moses so he could rest and then stood beside him, holding up his hands for the rest of the battle so that the Israelites would prevail. God could have let the Israelites win without Moses' hands in the air. But perhaps God chose to accomplish it this way so that we would appreciate the value of a helping hand.

There are just some things in this life that are too hard to do alone. Like Moses, we all need a helping hand from time to time. And when we allow others to help us, we are not the only ones who receive a blessing. Often when we allow someone to do something for us, they are blessed as much or more than we are. When you need help, don't be afraid to ask. Sometimes it can mean the difference between victory and defeat.

*For everything we know about God's Word is summed*
*up in a single sentence: Love others as you love yourself.*
GALATIANS 5:14 MSG

◆

*Finally, all of you be of one mind, having compassion for one*
*another; love as brothers, be tenderhearted, be courteous.*
1 PETER 3:8 NKJV

◆

*You do well when you complete the Royal Rule of*
*the Scriptures: "Love others as you love yourself."*
JAMES 2:8 MSG

◆

*Anyone who hates a brother or sister is a murderer, and you*
*know very well that eternal life and murder don't go together.*
1 JOHN 3:15 MSG

◆

*Work at living in peace with everyone, and work at living a*
*holy life, for those who are not holy will not see the Lord.*
HEBREWS 12:14 NLT

◆

*Therefore let us pursue the things which make for peace*
*and the things by which one may edify another.*
ROMANS 14:19 NKJV

*Love is patient, love is kind. It does not envy, it does not boast, it is not proud. It does not dishonor others, it is not self-seeking, it is not easily angered, it keeps no record of wrongs.*

1 CORINTHIANS 13:4–5 NIV

*"You shall not take vengeance, nor bear any grudge against the children of your people, but you shall love your neighbor as yourself."*

LEVITICUS 19:18 NKJV

*My beloved friends, let us continue to love each other since love comes from God. Everyone who loves is born of God and experiences a relationship with God.*

1 JOHN 4:7 MSG

*Share each other's burdens, and in this way obey the law of Christ.*

GALATIANS 6:2 NLT

*"You have heard the law that says, 'Love your neighbor' and hate your enemy. But I say, love your enemies! Pray for those who persecute you!"*

MATTHEW 5:43–44 NLT

*Rejoice with those who rejoice;*
*mourn with those who mourn.*

ROMANS 12:15 NIV

◆

*For this is the message you heard from the beginning:*
*We should love one another.*

1 JOHN 3:11 NIV

◆

*Respect everyone, and love the family of believers.*
*Fear God, and respect the king.*

1 PETER 2:17 NLT

◆

*"So if you are presenting a sacrifice at the altar in the*
*Temple and you suddenly remember that someone has*
*something against you, leave your sacrifice there at*
*the altar. Go and be reconciled to that person.*
*Then come and offer your sacrifice to God."*

MATTHEW 5:23–24 NLT

◆

*If it is possible, as much as depends on you,*
*live peaceably with all men.*

ROMANS 12:18 NKJV

# Making the Big Bucks: Managing Money

**H**ow exciting it is to earn a paycheck! Money, however, can become a major source of stress if it is mismanaged. The loss of a good credit record will limit purchases that may be made in the future. Arguments about money are known to contribute to the breakdown of marriages. So it is important to be proactive in your approach to finances. Most adults would agree that money management is a skill they wish they had acquired sooner!

Are you a college student working to pay for coursework or to earn spending money? Maybe you're a recent graduate who is entering the workforce, and you will be covering all of your own expenses for the first time. Regardless of your situation, applying basic financial-management principles is essential.

Principle number one is to tithe to your church. God promises to faithfully provide for His children when we are faithful in our tithing. He tells us in Malachi that He will "open the floodgates of heaven and pour out so much blessing that there will not be room enough to store it" (Malachi 3:10 NIV). If your church provides offering envelopes, put your tithe in an envelope on the day you get your paycheck. Take it to church on the following Sunday and enjoy the blessing of giving. Giving is an act of worship, just as much so as singing or praising God. We bring Him glory and honor through giving to His kingdom work. The Bible tells us that the Lord delights in a cheerful giver.

Managing finances involves budgeting. Choose one of the many online financial programs to help you design a personal budget and keep track of your spending online. It is a good idea to record all spending for a couple of months and use this information to design a budget that includes:

- tithe
- housing
- utilities
- food
- entertainment
- clothing
- miscellaneous

Each person will have a unique budget. Typically, about one-third of your paycheck will cover your rent or mortgage payment. Utility bills will vary, depending on the type of home you live in, the time of year, and your lifestyle. Request an average bill for your apartment or house before you even move into it. What can you do to keep your electricity bill low? Such things as turning off lights and not running heat or air-conditioning excessively can help with this.

Many money experts suggest saving $1,000 and placing it in a separate emergency account. When unexpected needs arise (and they always will), such as new tires for your car or dental work, your monthly budget will not be affected. When you use funds from your emergency account, replenish this "safety net" quickly. Be sure to use the money from this account only for true emergencies.

Managing finances, while it will come more naturally to some than others, can actually be rewarding and even fun!

*"Bring the whole tithe into the storehouse, so that there
may be food in My house, and test Me now in this," says
the LORD of hosts, "if I will not open for you the windows of
heaven and pour out for you a blessing until it overflows."*
MALACHI 3:10 NASB

◆

*Whoever loves money never has enough;
whoever loves wealth is never satisfied with
their income. This too is meaningless.*
ECCLESIASTES 5:10 NIV

◆

Avoid impulse purchases.
Plan ahead before you spend.

◆

*"Do not store up for yourselves treasures on earth, where
moth and rust destroy, and where thieves break in and steal.
But store up for yourselves treasures in heaven, where neither
moth nor rust destroys, and where thieves do not break in or
steal; for where your treasure is, there your heart will be also."*
MATTHEW 6:19–21 NASB

◆

*Dishonest money dwindles away, but whoever
gathers money little by little makes it grow.*
PROVERBS 13:11 NIV

Look for inexpensive or even free events in
your community. There are music festivals,
arts and crafts fairs, cultural events, and outdoor
concerts throughout the year in most cities.

◆

After college, even though I had avoided credit cards,
I still had a lot of debt: school loans, a car loan, wedding
bills, and a mortgage. I wanted to get rid of as much of it
as I could as fast as possible. It was so tempting to put my
extra money toward my smaller debts—the ones I could
pay off the fastest—but a good friend explained to me that
a better strategy is to pay off the debt with the highest
interest rate first. I did the math and realized this was
right—in the long run, I'd ultimately be saving more
money by following that advice.

ASHLEY CASTEEL, 23

◆

*"No one can serve two masters. Either you will hate the one
and love the other, or you will be devoted to the one and
despise the other. You cannot serve both God and money."*

LUKE 16:13 NIV

Little things can make a big difference in your budget. For example, purchasing twelve-packs of soft drinks rather than buying that soda for $1 each day from a machine can save you up to $7 per week, which is $28 per month and $336 per year.

◆

*Let no debt remain outstanding, except the continuing debt to love one another, for whoever loves others has fulfilled the law.*
ROMANS 13:8 NIV

◆

If you are a college or graduate student, ask your bank about a student checking account. Banks often waive certain fees and offer special benefits for students.

◆

*Once I was young, and now I am old. Yet I have never seen the godly abandoned or their children begging for bread. The godly always give generous loans to others, and their children are a blessing.*
PSALM 37:25–26 NLT

◆

Cooking at home with friends can be a lot of fun. It also saves money. Eating out really adds up if you do it too often.

# God's Gift of Health

*Do you not know that your bodies are temples of the Holy Spirit, who is in you, whom you have received from God? You are not your own; you were bought at a price. Therefore honor God with your bodies.*

1 CORINTHIANS 6:19–20 NIV

Our bodies are an amazing gift from God. But these incredible bodies aren't maintenance free. Just as we are to be good stewards of our resources of time and money, we should also be good stewards of our bodies. God's Word calls our bodies His temple.

When we are young, our bodies function so well that many of us make the mistake of abusing them. We exercise too much (or not enough), make poor food choices, and try to operate on too little sleep. If you're living this way now, you may still not realize the toll your lifestyle is taking on your body, but someday it might be too late to reverse some of the results!

God designed our earthly bodies to work for us for many, many years. That's why it's important to treat them with care and respect. Good habits like regular, moderate exercise, quality nutrition, and adequate sleep are simple things, but they pay enormous dividends. Honor God with your body and it will reward you by functioning precisely as the amazing creation God designed it to be.

*"Physical training is good, but training for godliness is much better, promising benefits in this life and in the life to come."*

1 TIMOTHY 4:8 NLT

*Dear friend, I hope all is well with you and that you are as healthy in body as you are strong in spirit.*

3 JOHN 1:2 NLT

*You don't know the first thing about tomorrow. You're nothing but a wisp of fog, catching a brief bit of sun before disappearing. Instead, make it a habit to say, "If the Master wills it and we're still alive, we'll do this or that."*

JAMES 4:14–15 MSG

*Charm can mislead and beauty soon fades. The woman to be admired and praised is the woman who lives in the Fear-of-God.*

PROVERBS 31:30 MSG

*"The LORD does not look at the things people look at. People look at the outward appearance, but the LORD looks at the heart."*

1 SAMUEL 16:7 NIV

*Therefore, if anyone is in Christ, he is a new creation;*
*old things have passed away;*
*behold, all things have become new.*

2 CORINTHIANS 5:17 NKJV

◆

*"Do not judge according to appearance,*
*but judge with righteous judgment."*

JOHN 7:24 NKJV

◆

*I also want the women to dress modestly, with decency*
*and propriety...not with elaborate hairstyles or gold*
*or pearls or expensive clothes, but with good deeds,*
*appropriate for women who profess to worship God.*

1 TIMOTHY 2:9–10 NIV

◆

*And so, dear brothers and sisters, I plead with you to*
*give your bodies to God.... Let them be a living and holy*
*sacrifice—the kind he will find acceptable.... Don't copy*
*the behavior and customs of this world, but let God*
*transform you into a new person by changing the way you*
*think. Then you will learn to know God's will for you,*
*which is good and pleasing and perfect.*

ROMANS 12:1–2 NLT

*There is no soundness in my flesh because of Your anger,*
*nor any health in my bones because of my sin.*
PSALM 38:3 NKJV

◆

*Since we have these promises, dear friends, let us purify*
*ourselves from everything that contaminates body*
*and spirit, perfecting holiness out of reverence for God.*
2 CORINTHIANS 7:1 NIV

◆

*Have mercy on me, O LORD, for I am weak;*
*O LORD, heal me, for my bones are troubled.*
PSALM 6:2 NKJV

◆

*Oh yes, you shaped me first inside, then out; you formed*
*me in my mother's womb. I thank you, High God—you're*
*breathtaking! Body and soul, I am marvelously made!*
PSALM 139:13–14 MSG

◆

*"No wonder my heart is glad, and my tongue*
*shouts his praises! My body rests in hope."*
ACTS 2:26 NLT

◆

*Remember that your bodies are created*
*with the same dignity as the Master's body.*
1 CORINTHIANS 6:15 MSG

# Talking with My Heavenly Father: Prayer

How many text messages and e-mails do you send in an average week? More than a hundred? Technology allows us to communicate constantly with our friends and family members. Cell phones and computers are wonderful tools for staying connected even with faraway loved ones.

Think about your communication with God. Is it as frequent? The Bible tells us to "pray continually." Do you spend time with God? Do you talk with Him, listen to Him, and seek Him in all things? It's easy to get so busy that prayer loses its priority in your life. God is pleased when you put relating to Him high on your list.

Have you set a particular time and place to meet with God on a regular basis? If you find it hard to focus during prayer times, you might try the ACTS acronym.

Express *adoration.* Praise God. This is different from *thanking* God in that adoration is telling God how much He means to you, not for what He has done but simply for *who He is.* Try praising the Lord by speaking scripture back to Him:

"God, You are the same yesterday, today, and tomorrow. Holy, holy, holy is the Lord God Almighty. You are above all things. You are perfect in every way."

Praise Him by speaking His names:

"Heavenly Father, Creator, God, Jehovah, my Jesus,

Emmanuel—God with us, the Great I Am, Savior, Yahweh."

Next, *confess* your sins to God. God already knows your sins, but it is good to come before Him and willingly confess your sins. Agree with God that sin hinders your fellowship with Him and with others. He is a *loving Father* who is so willing to forgive you when you ask. At the same time, He is a *holy God*. He calls believers to confess their sins and to turn from them, daily seeking to be more like Jesus.

After confession, express *thanksgiving* to God. Thank Him for the blessings He has poured out on you. Thank Him for His provisions His gifts, and for your salvation through Jesus' blood that was shed for you on the cross.

Finally, *supplication* is presenting your requests to God. You can pray for your own needs and for the needs of others. There will be times when you may not even know what to pray. The Bible assures us that the Holy Spirit prays for us at such times. Simply speak the name of Jesus. Present your requests to the Lord. Cast your cares upon Him.

Remember to be still before the Lord. If you do all the talking, God does not have a chance to work in your spirit. Some of the greatest direction and comfort come to God's children when they take time to rest in Him and listen for His still, small voice.

*The LORD is far from the wicked,*
*but he hears the prayer of the righteous.*
PROVERBS 15:29 NIV

God does not need your prayers to be filled
with ornate language. He is interested in
a humble heart and a sweet spirit.

*In the morning, LORD, you hear my voice; in the morning*
*I lay my requests before you and wait expectantly.*
PSALM 5:3 NIV

When you tell a friend that you will pray for him
or her, follow through with your promise. In fact,
ask if you can pray for the need right then and there.
Just stop wherever you are and pray over your friend.
There is great power in agreeing in prayer.

*The LORD detests the sacrifice of the wicked,*
*but the prayer of the upright pleases him.*
PROVERBS 15:8 NIV

*Now when Daniel learned that the decree had been
published, he went home to his upstairs room where the
windows opened toward Jerusalem. Three times a day
he got down on his knees and prayed, giving thanks
to his God, just as he had done before.*
DANIEL 6:10 NIV

◆

There is not a set time, date, or place to talk to God. Talk to
Him constantly and as personally as your best friend.
EMILY HOERNSCHEMEYER, 20

◆

*Rejoice always, pray continually, give thanks in all
circumstances; for this is God's will for you in Christ Jesus.*
1 THESSALONIANS 5:16–18 NIV

◆

*The effectual fervent prayer of
a righteous man availeth much.*
JAMES 5:16 KJV

◆

*"And when you pray, do not keep on babbling like pagans,
for they think they will be heard because of their many
words. Do not be like them, for your Father knows
what you need before you ask him."*
MATTHEW 6:7–8 NIV

# TURNING WORRY INTO PRAYER

*So let us come boldly to the throne of our gracious God.*
*There we will receive his mercy, and we will find*
*grace to help us when we need it most.*

HEBREWS 4:16 NLT

◆

Michael was worried. It had been weeks since he applied to graduate school, and he still hadn't heard a thing. What if he didn't get accepted into his program? Then he'd have to start paying back student loans right away. What if he couldn't get a job because he lacked experience? What if he would never be able to move out of his parents' house? Before long Michael would break out in a sweat, sure he was doomed to flip burgers for the rest of his life.

Sound familiar? When we get carried away with worry, it becomes like a runaway freight train, gaining speed and momentum at every turn. No matter what worries you, the next time you are overcome with worry, instead of getting carried away with what-ifs, turn that worry into a prayer. Then relax and take a deep breath. You can be sure that your worries and your future are safe with God.

*Are any of you suffering hardships? You should pray.*
*Are any of you happy? You should sing praises.*
JAMES 5:13 NLT

*Because of Christ and our faith in him, we can now come*
*boldly and confidently into God's presence.*
EPHESIANS 3:12 NLT

*We're bold and free before God! We're able to stretch*
*our hands out and receive what we asked for because*
*we're doing what he said, doing what pleases him.*
1 JOHN 3:21-22 MSG

*Don't quit in hard times; pray all the harder.*
ROMANS 12:12 MSG

*Is anyone among you sick? Let them call the elders of the*
*church to pray over them and anoint him with oil in the*
*name of the Lord. And the prayer offered in faith will*
*make the sick person well; the Lord will raise them up.*
*If they have sinned, they will be forgiven.*
JAMES 5:14-15 NIV

*I desire therefore that the men pray everywhere,*
*lifting up holy hands, without wrath and doubting.*
1 TIMOTHY 2:8 NKJV

◆

*"If you, then, though you are evil, know how to give good*
*gifts to your children, how much more will your Father*
*in heaven give good gifts to those who ask him!"*
MATTHEW 7:11 NIV

◆

*The moment we get tired in the waiting, God's Spirit is right*
*alongside helping us along. If we don't know how or what to*
*pray, it doesn't matter. He does our praying in and for us,*
*making prayer out of our wordless sighs, our aching groans.*
ROMANS 8:26 MSG

◆

*The Lord is near to all who call on him,*
*to all who call on him in truth.*
PSALM 145:18 NIV

*"Therefore I say to you, whatever things you ask when you pray, believe that you receive them, and you will have them."*

MARK 11:24 NKJV

◆

*"When you call on me, when you come and pray to me, I'll listen. When you come looking for me, you'll find me."*

JEREMIAH 29:12–13 MSG

◆

*"You haven't done this before. Ask, using my name, and you will receive, and you will have abundant joy."*

JOHN 16:24 NLT

◆

*"Before they call I will answer; while they are still speaking I will hear."*

ISAIAH 65:24 NIV

◆

*"Ask, and it will be given to you; seek, and you will find; knock, and it will be opened to you."*

MATTHEW 7:7 NKJV

# Make Me a Servant: Serving Others

When I was in school, it was so easy to find service projects to get involved in. The bloodmobile came to campus and some of my classes were organized around service projects. There were always weekend trips the school offered to nursing homes, churches, and schools. I never had to go out of my way to serve others. It wasn't until I graduated that I realized how much I had taken that for granted. Now I have to work around my work schedule, finances, and find my own ways to serve—but in many ways that makes the service work I'm doing now much more personally fulfilling.

ASHLEY CASTEEL, 23

The word *service* shows up in church a lot. The pastor asks for us to serve in the nursery. The bulletin advertises a need for people to serve as parking attendants and children's choir directors. Missionaries serve in Africa, China, and even right here at home in our own country. *Serving* is used in other contexts also. We serve food to guests and tennis balls to opponents. So what does *service* mean, and what does it have to do with you?

Christ Jesus taught that the least would be greatest. He modeled putting others ahead of Himself. He washed feet; turned water to wine; and helped, healed, and blessed those He came into contact with everywhere. He was a King, and yet He didn't come to earth demanding a palace and a throne. Our Savior came to us as Emmanuel, meaning "God with us." He came humbly, served humbly, and loved people with a greater love than this world had ever known.

So, how can you follow Jesus' example? How can you be a servant? After all, your schedule is packed. You may have classes as well as a full- or part-time job. You are juggling a professional and a personal life. You are new at the office and expected to put in a lot of extra hours.

Serving can be simple. Start small and choose an area that interests you where you can start serving. God has made you unique in your personality, strengths, and passions. If you love animals, use this to help others. There are ministries in many communities and churches that take dogs and puppies into nursing homes or hospitals to cheer the patients. Do you enjoy working with children? There is always a need for childcare so that parents can attend services and Bible classes in church or at apartment ministries. Serving can mean visiting a homebound friend or filling soup bowls at a homeless shelter. It will grow as you discover the blessings of being a servant for the kingdom of Jesus. You may one day start a new ministry in your church or establish a Bible study at your company! But even the smallest acts of service never go unnoticed by God, and you will be richly blessed through the act of giving to others.

*God, thank You for opportunities to serve You by serving others. Give me a servant's heart, I pray. Amen.*

*"So when you give to the needy, do not announce it with trumpets, as the hypocrites do in the synagogues and on the streets, to be honored by others. Truly I tell you, they have received their reward in full. But when you give to the needy, do not let your left hand know what your right hand is doing, so that your giving may be in secret. Then your Father, who sees what is done in secret, will reward you."*

MATTHEW 6:2–4 NIV

◆

Make a habit of thanking those who serve *you.* Waiters, store clerks, teachers, families, and custodians need to know that you appreciate their service.

◆

*"A new command I give you: Love one another. As I have loved you, so you must love one another. By this everyone will know that you are my disciples, if you love one another."*

JOHN 13:34–35 NIV

◆

*The entire law is fulfilled in keeping this one command: "Love your neighbor as yourself."*

GALATIANS 5:14 NIV

Service involves time. To serve requires that you trade in some "you time" and make it "others time." Do you have a free hour or two per week? Serve the Lord. It will become the time of your week that you look forward to the most!

◆

*Pure and undefiled religion in the sight of our God and Father is this: to visit orphans and widows in their distress, and to keep oneself unstained by the world.*
JAMES 1:27 NASB

◆

Serve for the sake of love, for the sake of service— not for a pat on the back or a thank-you. Service done in secret is especially pleasing to the Lord.

◆

*If anyone serves, they should do so with the strength God provides, so that in all things God may be praised through Jesus Christ. To him be the glory and the power for ever and ever. Amen.*
1 PETER 4:11 NIV

Serve those whom you work with on a daily basis.
Fill a coffee cup. Cover a class. Pick up a shift.
Share a word of encouragement. In doing so,
you may be the only Jesus that coworker ever sees.

◆

*You, my brothers and sisters, were called to be free. But do
not use your freedom to indulge the flesh; rather, serve one
another humbly in love. For the entire law fulfilled in keeping
this one command: "Love your neighbor as yourself."*
GALATIANS 5:13-14 NIV

◆

*Jesus called them together and said, "...Whoever
wants to become great among you must be your servant,
and whoever wants to be first must be your slave—
just as the Son of Man did not come to be served,
but to serve, and to give his life as a ransom for many."*
MATTHEW 20:25-28 NIV

◆

*Each of you should use whatever gift you have
received to serve others, as faithful stewards
of God's grace in its various forms.*
1 PETER 4:10 NIV

# A Giving Heart

*"Give, and you will receive. Your gift will return to you in full—pressed down, shaken together to make room for more, running over, and poured into your lap. The amount you give will determine the amount you get back."*

LUKE 6:38 NLT

After four hard years of college, Greg landed his dream job and finally made enough money to live on his own. As he sat down with his dad to review his budget, he was proud to show that there was enough to cover rent, insurance, and even a little spending money.

"What about your tithe?" Greg's dad asked.

"Well, uh...I guess I was just thinking I'd wait until I made a little more money...." Greg stumbled.

"Over the years I've learned to set my tithe aside before paying for anything else," his dad said. "As a result, I've discovered that God is always faithful to meet my needs—and more. Don't sell yourself short, Greg. You can swing it."

Greg decided to follow his dad's advice, and amazingly, he had more than enough money to meet his needs.

God's economy is different from the world's. The principle is to give a portion of what God has already blessed you with. In return He promises to meet your every need and more. As you embark on a new stage of life, start putting God first in your finances. You won't regret it.

*A good name is to be chosen rather than great riches,
loving favor rather than silver and gold.*

PROVERBS 22:1 NKJV

◆

*But remember the LORD your God, for it is he who gives you
the ability to produce wealth, and so confirms his covenant,
which he swore to your ancestors, as it is today.*

DEUTERONOMY 8:18 NIV

◆

*Honor the LORD with your wealth and with the best part of
everything you produce. Then he will fill your barns with
grain, and your vats will overflow with good wine.*

PROVERBS 3:9–10 NLT

◆

*Don't be obsessed with getting more material things.
Be relaxed with what you have. Since God assured us,
"I'll never let you down, never walk off and leave you."*

HEBREWS 13:5 MSG

◆

*"Every man shall give as he is able, according to the
blessing of the LORD your God which He has given you."*

DEUTERONOMY 16:17 NKJV

*But those who desire to be rich fall into temptation and a snare, and into many foolish and harmful lusts which drown men in destruction and perdition. For the love of money is a root of all kinds of evil, for which some have strayed from the faith in their greediness, and pierced themselves through with many sorrows.*

1 TIMOTHY 6:9–11 NKJV

*"Here's the lesson: Use your worldly resources to benefit others and make friends. Then, when your earthly possessions are gone, they will welcome you to an eternal home."*

LUKE 16:9 NLT

*Trust in your money and down you go!*
*But the godly flourish like leaves in spring.*

PROVERBS 11:28 NLT

*"You can't worship two gods at once. Loving one god, you'll end up hating the other. Adoration of one feeds contempt for the other. You can't worship God and Money both."*

MATTHEW 6:24 MSG

*I have seen a grievous evil under the sun: wealth hoarded to the harm of its owners, or wealth lost through some misfortune, so that when they have children there is nothing left for them to inherit. Everyone comes naked from their mother's womb, and as everyone comes, so they depart. They take nothing from their toil that they can carry in their hands.*

ECCLESIASTES 5:13–15 NIV

*Command those who are rich in this present world not to be arrogant nor to put their hope in wealth, which is so uncertain, but to put their hope in God, who richly provides us with everything for our enjoyment.*

1 TIMOTHY 6:17 NIV

*Speaking to the people, [Jesus] went on, "Take care! Protect yourself against the least bit of greed. Life is not defined by what you have, even when you have a lot."*

LUKE 12:15 MSG

*So let each one give as he purposes in his heart, not
grudgingly or of necessity; for God loves a cheerful giver.*
2 CORINTHIANS 9:7 NKJV

◆

*Believers who are poor have something to boast about,
for God has honored them. And those who are rich
should boast that God has humbled them.*
JAMES 1:9–10 NLT

◆

*"Do not store up for yourselves treasures on earth, where
moth and vermin destroy, and where thieves break in and
steal. But store up for yourselves treasures in heaven. . . .
For where your treasure is, there your heart will be also."*
MATTHEW 6:19–21 NIV

◆

*Since we entered the world penniless and
will leave it penniless, if we have bread on the
table and shoes on our feet, that's enough.*
1 TIMOTHY 6:7–8 MSG

# Playing Nice: The Importance of Forgiveness

I've been reminded many times throughout my college years of God's command to forgive, no matter how badly the grievance has hurt you. It can be extremely difficult, but in the end, the relationship is always stronger, and the forgiveness is always worth it—especially if the other person is your roommate or hall mate.

AMANDA WEIDMAN, 21

*race.* It is a word we sing about. It is in many well-known songs and hymns. It is a word that is present in many scriptures that even young children memorize in Sunday school classes. Do we really grasp its meaning, though? What is grace?

Grace has been defined as "unmerited favor." It is not earned. It is a gift. God demonstrated amazing grace when He sacrificed His only Son, Jesus, for us on the cross. Through Jesus, we are forgiven of our sins. Ephesians 2:8–9 (NIV) says, "It is by grace you have been saved. . .not by works, so that no one can boast." We do not do anything to achieve salvation other than to believe and accept God's grace.

We have been shown grace. And it's because we have been shown this grace that we must also show it to others. It is not always easy to forgive. Intentionally or unintentionally, others will hurt us—it's a fact. Some level of hurt, rejection, and disappointment is inevitable if we are to exist in relationship with others. So it is so important that we learn to forgive.

Forgiveness does not mean that you accept what was done to you and agree that it was okay. In fact, it is quite the opposite. It means that although you *know* what was done to you was not right, you *choose* to pardon the offender. You choose to be merciful.

The Bible is very clear about forgiveness. Jesus said that we should forgive our neighbors seventy times seven, implying that our forgiveness should be unlimited. As Christians, we should be known as those who are quick to forgive, setting an example for others.

In your work, with your family and friends, and as you live in and among others in your community, you will encounter times when you can forgive or you can get angry, gossip, and claim your rights as the victim. One option will tie you down in bitterness, while the other will free you to live life unencumbered. Choose forgiveness. It is always the best choice.

*Father, I have been forgiven much.*
*Help me, in turn, to forgive. Amen.*

Satan despises forgiveness. There's nothing he likes more than to see God's children involved in disagreements. Satan is all about barriers and selfishness. Jesus is all about selflessness and forgiveness. Whom will you honor with your choices when it comes to forgiving others— the prince of this world or the Prince of Peace?

◆

*Then Peter came and said to Him, "Lord, how often shall my brother sin against me and I forgive him? Up to seven times?" Jesus said to him, "I do not say to you, up to seven times, but up to seventy times seven."*
MATTHEW 18:21–22 NASB

◆

*When we were overwhelmed by sins, you forgave our transgressions.*
PSALM 65:3 NIV

◆

*"Forgive us our sins, as we have forgiven those who sin against us."*
MATTHEW 6:12 NLT

*Sensible people control their temper;*
*they earn respect by overlooking wrongs.*
PROVERBS 19:11 NLT

◆

When you find it hard to forgive, pray that
God will give you a heart of forgiveness.

◆

*Above all, love each other deeply,*
*because love covers over a multitude of sins.*
1 PETER 4:8 NIV

◆

*"Do not condemn, and you will not be condemned.*
*Forgive, and you will be forgiven. Give, and it will be given to*
*you. A good measure, pressed down, shaken together*
*and running over, will be poured into your lap. For with*
*the measure you use, it will be measured to you."*
LUKE 6:37–38 NIV

◆

*As far as the east is from the west, so far*
*has he removed our transgressions from us.*
PSALM 103:12 NIV

# THE GIFT THAT KEEPS ON GIVING

*"But when you are praying, first forgive anyone you
are holding a grudge against, so that your
Father in heaven will forgive your sins, too."*

MARK 11:25 NLT

K im couldn't decide what hurt more: the fact that her boyfriend broke up with her or the fact that he was dating someone else while they were together. More than anything, Kim struggled to forgive her ex-boyfriend.

Friends encouraged her to vent her feelings and assured her it would help her heal. But even after months of venting her anger, Kim still didn't feel any better. In fact, she began to wonder if she was getting worse.

Maybe you can relate to Kim. Perhaps someone you once loved has betrayed you beyond what you feel you can forgive. If you feel this way, know that God understands. He knows what it feels like to be betrayed and rejected by us. And yet He forgives us again and again—a gift that is ours for the asking. Because we experience His never-ending forgiveness, He asks us to offer the same gift to others. The truth is, you can't forgive on your own strength. Ask God for help, and He'll be there to fill you with a spirit of forgiveness.

*"You have heard that it was said, 'Eye for eye, and tooth for tooth.' But I tell you, do not resist an evil person. If anyone slaps you on the right cheek, turn to them the other cheek also."*

MATTHEW 5:38-39 NIV

◆

*Where is another God like you, who pardons the guilt of the remnant, overlooking the sins of his special people? You will not stay angry with your people forever, because you delight in showing unfailing love.*

MICAH 7:18 NLT

◆

*O my soul, bless GOD, don't forget a single blessing! He forgives your sins—every one. He heals your diseases—every one.*

PSALM 103:2-3 MSG

◆

*"None of the sins that person has committed will be remembered against them. They have done what is just and right; they will surely live."*

EZEKIEL 33:16 NIV

◆

*Have mercy on me, O God, because of your unfailing love. Because of your great compassion, blot out the stain of my sins.*

PSALM 51:1 NLT

*This is my blood, God's new covenant poured
out for many people for the forgiveness of sins.*
MATTHEW 26:28 MSG

◆

*Instead, be kind to each other, tenderhearted, forgiving one
another, just as God through Christ has forgiven you.*
EPHESIANS 4:32 NLT

◆

*Don't repay evil for evil. Don't retaliate with insults
when people insult you. Instead, pay them back with
a blessing. That is what God has called you to do,
and he will grant you his blessing.*
1 PETER 3:9 NLT

◆

*"If your brother sins against you, rebuke him; and if he
repents, forgive him. And if he sins against you seven
times in a day, and seven times in a day returns to you,
saying, 'I repent,' you shall forgive him."*
LUKE 17:3–4 NKJV

◆

*Make allowance for each other's faults, and forgive
anyone who offends you. Remember, the Lord
forgave you, so you must forgive others.*
COLOSSIANS 3:13 NLT

# Take a Deep Breath: Finding Peace

Peace is one of the most sought-after commodities in today's world. Some people try to find it in relationships, while others bury their troubles in alcohol or drugs. None of these things can truly deliver peace, but those who don't know Jesus can't see this. Sometimes even believers lose sight of the source of peace, but we must return to it if we are to live the abundant life God desires for us.

God grants a peace unlike any peace the world can offer. He freely gives a peace that passes all understanding, a deep abiding peace even in times of trouble. Have you ever witnessed a family that is dealing with a difficult trial, and yet faces it with amazing strength? That kind of strength is supernatural. It comes through faith in Christ. God's peace works the same way. There are no test results that can steal this type of peace. There is no bad news, rejection, or failure capable of robbing a heart that has the peace of Jesus.

For centuries, God's people have rested in peace at night despite circumstances that appeared unbearable. King David hid in caves and ran for his life, yet he found peace in the Lord. Noah was ridiculed for building an ark, but he just kept hammering. Armies have marched into battle under the banner of God's peace even when they fought against the strongest of enemies. We are no different today. We can choose peace in the face of pain and even uncertainty. God offers it. We must simply accept it—a free gift, just like His grace.

How do you find this peace? Breathe deep. Be still. Know that He is God. Your sovereign maker holds the entire universe in His hands. Surely He can manage the details of your dilemma and calm the confusion of your situation.

Peace is hard to find with music blaring, text messages ringing, and e-mails going out. Experiencing God while you are playing video games is tough. Seek solitude. Ask God to meet with you on the porch, in your prayer closet, or as you kneel beside your bed. Ask Him for rest, comfort, and for healing of the wounded parts of your spirit. Tell God you want Him to replace your rebellion with submission, your will with His, and your anxiety with His peace. Ask Him to hug you, to hold you. You will experience His peace as you read the Psalms, as you sing praise to Him, and as you quiet your soul before Him. Peace is a treasure. Value it as such, and you will never be without it again.

◆

*Jesus, my Prince of Peace, be my rest.*
*Be my peace. I need You so. Amen.*

*Oh, love the Lord, all you His saints! For the Lord preserves the faithful, and fully repays the proud person. Be of good courage, and He shall strengthen your heart, all you who hope in the Lord.*
PSALM 31:23–24 NKJV

*"Come to me, all you who are weary and burdened, and I will give you rest. Take my yoke upon you and learn from me, for I am gentle and humble in heart, and you will find rest for your souls. For my yoke is easy and my burden is light."*
MATTHEW 11:28–30 NIV

Peace cannot be purchased. It is free. It cannot be earned. It is yours for the taking. Ask your Abba Father, your Daddy, your loving God. . .and He will plant in your heart a peace that cannot be reckoned with. It is a gift. Stop searching. Accept it.

*In peace I will lie down and sleep, for you alone, Lord, make me dwell in safety.*
PSALM 4:8 NIV

*Do not be anxious about anything, but in every situation,
by prayer and petition, with thanksgiving, present
your requests to God. And the peace of God,
which transcends all understanding, will guard your
hearts and your minds in Christ Jesus.*

PHILIPPIANS 4:6-7 NIV

Peace is not found in the world. It is a rare and precious
gift that is apparent in the believer's life. True peace
cannot be experienced without Jesus in your heart.

*"The LORD bless you and keep you; the LORD make his
face shine on you and be gracious to you; the LORD
turn his face toward you and give you peace."*

NUMBERS 6:24-26 NIV

Can it be that peace is not understood, not fully, by one
who has never experienced unrest? To even once know
confusion reveals to a soul the opposite—the sweet,
calming peace of Jesus. To have been void of peace
causes us to savor its sweetness all the more.

You can't rush through your entire day and expect to sense God's peace. You must set aside time to rest in Him, talk with Him, and listen to Him. Only then will you find His peace that passes all understanding.

*Grace and peace to you from God our Father and the Lord Jesus Christ.*
PHILEMON 1:3 NIV

Pray for peace. World peace. National peace. Peace within your community, your workplace, your school. Pray for peace in your family and in your heart. God is the giver of all peace. Pray for it. Pray earnestly. He will hear you, and He will provide the peace you seek.

*Peacemakers who sow in peace reap a harvest of righteousness.*
JAMES 3:18 NIV

# PERFECT PEACE

*You will keep in perfect peace all who trust in you,*
*all whose thoughts are fixed on you!*
ISAIAH 26:3 NLT

◆

Suzanne was exhausted. Pressures at work had become increasingly intense, and each day she felt as if she was falling further and further behind. She desperately tried to pray about her situation, but after a while, the words just wouldn't come. She became so consumed by the details of her demanding job, she didn't know where to begin. She tossed and turned at night, wondering how she was going to get it all done.

Have you ever felt this way? Jesus understands that life can be busy and overwhelming. He knows that it sometimes seems like too much to bear. His advice in this regard is simple: do not worry about tomorrow; each day has enough trouble of its own. Looking too far ahead into the future—even one day—can paralyze us with worry and exhaustion, so much so that we don't feel like doing anything at all.

Jesus taught that it's far more effective to tackle life one step at a time. Not only does this keep our worry at a minimum, it also enables us to trust God to help us accomplish what we cannot do on our own. Living in the moment takes practice, but it's a worthwhile investment of your time.

*Now may the Lord of peace Himself give you peace*
*always in every way. The Lord be with you all.*
2 THESSALONIANS 3:16 NKJV

◆

*And let the peace of God rule in your hearts, to which*
*also you were called in one body; and be thankful.*
COLOSSIANS 3:15 NKJV

◆

*"But all who listen to me will live in peace,*
*untroubled by fear of harm."*
PROVERBS 1:33 NLT

◆

*"Behold, I will bring it health and healing; I will heal them*
*and reveal to them the abundance of peace and truth."*
JEREMIAH 33:6 NKJV

◆

*"Peace I leave with you; my peace I give you. I do not*
*give to you as the world gives. Do not let your*
*hearts be troubled and do not be afraid."*
JOHN 14:27 NIV

◆

*I waited patiently for the LORD to help me,*
*and he turned to me and heard my cry.*
PSALM 40:1 NLT

*Don't worry about anything; instead, pray about everything.*
*Tell God what you need, and thank him for all he has done.*
*Then you will experience God's peace, which exceeds*
*anything we can understand. His peace will guard your*
*hearts and minds as you live in Christ Jesus.*

PHILIPPIANS 4:6–7 NLT

*"Glory to God in the highest,*
*and on earth peace, goodwill toward men!"*

LUKE 2:14 NKJV

*"For even if the mountains walk away and the hills*
*fall to pieces, my love won't walk away from you,*
*my covenant commitment of peace won't fall apart."*
*The GOD who has compassion on you says so.*

ISAIAH 54:10 MSG

*May the God of hope fill you with all joy and peace*
*as you trust in him, so that you may overflow*
*with hope by the power of the Holy Spirit.*

ROMANS 15:13 NIV

*"I'll make a covenant of peace with them that will hold everything together, an everlasting covenant."*
EZEKIEL 37:26 MSG

*God doesn't stir us up into confusion;*
*he brings us into harmony.*
1 CORINTHIANS 14:33 MSG

*"These things I have spoken to you, that in Me you may have peace. In the world you will have tribulation; but be of good cheer, I have overcome the world."*
JOHN 16:33 NKJV

*So letting your sinful nature control your mind leads to death. But letting the Spirit control yourmind leads to life and peace.*
ROMANS 8:6 NLT

*GOD makes his people strong.*
*GOD gives his people peace.*
PSALM 29:11 MSG

# A Thankful Spirit

*Be thankful in all circumstances, for this is
God's will for you who belong to Christ Jesus.*

1 THESSALONIANS 5:18 NLT

ara was head cheerleader in high school and was known
for her perkiness and optimism. So when she tried out
for her college's cheer squad, she did so with the utmost
confidence. When the tryout results were posted, Sara
couldn't believe her name wasn't listed. She was deeply
disappointed as she tried to imagine surviving a whole
football season without cheerleading. Then her roommate
suggested Sara join her on Wednesday afternoons when she
volunteered as a reading tutor at a local community center.
Why not? It wasn't like she had anything better to do.

By the end of the school year, Sara wouldn't have
missed those Wednesday afternoons for anything. She
grew to love the children in a way she never would have
imagined and ended up changing her major to elementary
education. As she looked back, Sara found herself extremely
grateful she hadn't made the cheerleading squad—or she
might never have taken the opportunity to experience such
a rewarding activity.

When our plans don't work out, gratitude is not always
the first feeling that comes to mind. We might first become
frustrated, angry, disappointed, or humiliated. But the next
time Plan A doesn't work, try being grateful and wait to see
what God will do. More often than not, God's Plan B is more
wonderful than we could ever dream.

*Let me shout God's name with a praising song,*
*let me tell his greatness in a prayer of thanks.*
PSALM 69:30 MSG

◆

*And give thanks for everything to God the Father*
*in the name of our Lord Jesus Christ.*
EPHESIANS 5:20 NLT

◆

*In everything give thanks; for this is the*
*will of God in Christ Jesus for you.*
1 THESSALONIANS 5:18 NKJV

◆

*But thanks be to God, who gives us the*
*victory through our Lord Jesus Christ.*
1 CORINTHIANS 15:57 NKJV

◆

*Then he took the seven loaves and the fish, and when*
*he had given thanks, he broke them and gave them*
*to the disciples, and they in turn to the people.*
MATTHEW 15:36 NIV

*Let us come before His presence with thanksgiving;*
*let us shout joyfully to Him with psalms.*

PSALM 95:2 NKJV

◆

*In that wonderful day you will sing: "Thank the LORD!*
*Praise his name! Tell the nations what he has done.*
*Let them know how mighty he is!"*

ISAIAH 12:4 NLT

◆

*Give thanks to GOD—he is good and his love never quits.*

1 CHRONICLES 16:34 MSG

◆

*Are any of you suffering hardships? You should pray.*
*Are any of you happy? You should sing praises.*

JAMES 5:13 NLT

◆

*I will praise You, O LORD, with my whole heart;*
*I will tell of all Your marvelous works.*

PSALM 9:1 NKJV

◆

*"But I, with a song of grateful praise, will sacrifice to you.*
*What I have vowed I will make good. I will say,*
*'Salvation comes from the LORD.'"*

JONAH 2:9 NIV

*And whatever you do or say, do it as a representative of the
Lord Jesus, giving thanks through him to God the Father.*
COLOSSIANS 3:17 NLT

◆

*Do not be anxious about anything,
but in every situation, by prayer and petition,
with thanksgiving, present your requests to God.*
PHILIPPIANS 4:6 NIV

◆

*I urge, then, first of all, that petitions, prayers,
intercession and thanksgiving be made for all people.*
1 TIMOTHY 2:1 NIV

◆

*For all things are for your sakes, that grace,
having spread through the many, may cause
thanksgiving to abound to the glory of God.*
2 CORINTHIANS 4:15 NKJV

◆

*Sing to GOD a thanksgiving hymn,
play music on your instruments to God.*
PSALM 147:7 MSG

# True Honesty

*A friend loves at all times.*
PROVERBS 17:17 NIV

Katie sighed as she hung up the phone. It was her friend Christine—for the third time that week.

"I hope I'm not bothering you. . ." Christine began. "I *have* to talk to someone, and you always give such great advice. You don't mind, do you?"

Katie hesitated. In truth, Christine's constant phone calls were really starting to irritate her. But even though Christine was insensitive about interrupting and those phone calls often took up more than an hour, Katie didn't have the heart to tell her the truth. Instead she said, "Sure— I've got all the time you need." By the time the conversation was over, Katie's frustration was at an all-time high, and once again Christine didn't have a clue. Katie wished there was a way to let Christine know how she felt without losing the friendship, but she wasn't sure how to do it.

Telling the truth is often accompanied by consequences. When we are truthful with others, it can sometimes mean hurting their feelings or changing the relationship. But the Bible is clear: when we fail to speak the truth—in love—we are failing to live authentic lives and ultimately can do real damage to ourselves and others. Is there someone in your life with whom you are having difficulty telling the truth? What steps can you take today to be more truthful?

*Be completely humble and gentle; be patient,*
*bearing with one another in love.*
EPHESIANS 4:2 NIV

◆

*But you desire honesty from the womb,*
*teaching me wisdom even there.*
PSALM 51:6 NLT

◆

*The end of a thing is better than its beginning;*
*the patient in spirit is better than the proud in spirit.*
ECCLESIASTES 7:8 NKJV

◆

*We reject all shameful deeds and underhanded methods.*
*We don't try to trick anyone or distort the word of God. We*
*tell the truth before God, and all who are honest know this.*
2 CORINTHIANS 4:2 NLT

◆

*Pray for us, for our conscience is clear and we*
*want to live honorably in everything we do.*
HEBREWS 13:18 NLT

*Let integrity and uprightness preserve me,*
*for I wait for You.*

◆

*"Here is a simple, rule-of-thumb guide for behavior:*
*Ask yourself what you want people to do for you,*
*then grab the initiative and do it for them. Add up*
*God's Law and Prophets and this is what you get."*

MATTHEW 7:12 MSG

◆

*An honest answer is like a warm hug.*

PROVERBS 24:26 MSG

◆

*For we are taking pains to do what is right, not only*
*in the eyes of the Lord but also in the eyes of man.*

2 CORINTHIANS 8:21 NIV

◆

*"Do not lie. Do not deceive one another."*

LEVITICUS 19:11 NIV

◆

*The LORD detests the use of dishonest scales,*
*but he delights in accurate weights.*

PROVERBS 11:1 NLT

*God can't stomach liars; he loves the
company of those who keep their word.*
PROVERBS 12:22 MSG

◆

*Do not lie to each other, since you have taken off your old self
with its practices and have put on the new self, which is being
renewed in knowledge in the image of its Creator.*
COLOSSIANS 3:9–10 NIV

◆

*Mark the blameless man, and observe the upright;
for the future of that man is peace.*
PSALM 37:37 NKJV

◆

*He who speaks truth declares righteousness,
but a false witness, deceit.*
PROVERBS 12:17 NKJV

◆

*Buy truth—don't sell it for love or money;
buy wisdom, buy education, buy insight.*
PROVERBS 23:23 MSG

## Everlasting Hope

*You, Lord, are my lamp; the Lord*
*turns my darkness into light.*
2 SAMUEL 22:29 NIV

◆

The Bible begins with light. Genesis 1:3 (NIV) tells us, "And God said, 'Let there be light,' and there was light." It also ends with light. Revelation 22:5 (NIV) says, "There will be no more night. They will not need the light of a lamp or the light of the sun, for the Lord God will give them light."

Unfortunately, there's a lot of darkness in between. War. Murder. Pain. Loss. But even in the midst of the darkness there are glorious glimpses of His marvelous light. David's sin is forgiven and he becomes a man after God's own heart. Paul is transformed from a murderer of Christians to a passionate evangelist. Peter denied Christ, but that wasn't his destiny—instead he defends Christ to the death. God has the amazing ability to turn even our darkest situations into personal and spiritual victories.

Perhaps you are facing a dark situation right now. Maybe you've suffered loss, a moral failure, or missed a chance to defend your faith. If so, you're not alone. When it seems that you're surrounded by darkness, remember that light is both your foundation and your future. Release the situation to His marvelous light and know that He is able to transform it into something beautiful.

*"The people who sat in darkness have seen a great light. And for those who lived in the land where death casts its shadow, a light has shined."*

MATTHEW 4:16 NLT

◆

*The LORD is my light and my salvation; whom shall I fear? The LORD is the strength of my life; of whom shall I be afraid?*

PSALM 27:1 NKJV

◆

*"He uncovers mysteries hidden in darkness; he brings light to the deepest gloom."*

JOB 12:22 NLT

◆

*Send out your light and your truth; let them guide me. Let them lead me to your holy mountain, to the place where you live.*

PSALM 43:3 NLT

◆

*But if we walk in the light, as he is in the light, we have fellowship with one another, and the blood of Jesus, his Son, purifies us from all sin.*

1 JOHN 1:7 NIV

*His brightness was like the light; He had rays flashing
from His hand, and there His power was hidden.*

◆

*"For as long as I am in the world, there is
plenty of light. I am the world's Light."*
JOHN 9:5 MSG

◆

*For the LORD God is a sun and shield; the LORD will
give grace and glory; no good thing will He
withhold from those who walk uprightly.*
PSALM 84:11 NKJV

◆

*In him was life, and that life was the light of all mankind.*
JOHN 1:4 NIV

◆

*Let the light of your face shine on us.*
PSALM 4:6 NIV

◆

*Oh, how sweet the light of day,
and how wonderful to live in the sunshine!*
ECCLESIASTES 11:7 MSG

*The City doesn't need sun or moon for light.*
*God's Glory is its light, the Lamb its lamp!*
REVELATION 21:23 MSG

◆

*God said, "Light up the darkness!" and our lives filled*
*up with light as we saw and understood God in*
*the face of Christ, all bright and beautiful.*
2 CORINTHIANS 4:6 MSG

◆

*But you are not like that, for you are a chosen people.*
*You are royal priests, a holy nation, God's very own*
*possession. As a result, you can show others the*
*goodness of God, for he called you out of the darkness*
*into his wonderful light.*
1 PETER 2:9 NLT

◆

*The precepts of the LORD are right, giving joy*
*to the heart. The commands of the LORD*
*are radiant, giving light to the eyes.*
PSALM 19:8 NIV

# I've Got the Joy

*I know what it is to be in need, and I know what it is to have plenty. I have learned the secret of being content in any and every situation, whether well fed or hungry, whether living in plenty or in want.*

PHILIPPIANS 4:12 NIV

Since Paul traveled extensively throughout the Mediterranean, he could have easily penned Philippians 4:12 from a tranquil seaside villa. The truth is that he was confined to a dark and lifeless prison cell when he wrote it. It's one thing to be content when we're basking in the sun, quite another thing when life is falling apart at the seams.

The secret to contentment and joy, as Paul discovered, is twofold. One is to realize that even good situations can change on a dime. One day you can be sailing on clear blue waters and the next day be tossed about in the perfect storm. We are wise to remember that our circumstances—good or bad—will not last forever.

The second part is knowing you're never alone. Although human strength doesn't travel from calm to turbulent waters very smoothly, the One who walked on water is quite comfortable in the storm. He'll never leave you.

Decide to find joy and contentment in Jesus today.

*The LORD is my strength and my shield; my heart trusted in*
*Him, and I am helped; therefore my heart greatly rejoices,*
*and with my song I will praise Him.*
PSALM 28:7 NKJV

◆

*"You will go out in joy and be led forth in peace;*
*the mountains and hills will burst into song before you,*
*and all the trees of the field will clap their hands."*
ISAIAH 55:12 NIV

◆

*Be joyful in hope, patient in affliction, faithful in prayer.*
ROMANS 12:12 NIV

◆

*"You have made known to me the ways of life;*
*You will make me full of joy in Your presence."*
ACTS 2:28 NKJV

◆

*Those who plant in tears will harvest with shouts of joy.*
*They weep as they go to plant their seed,*
*but they sing as they return with the harvest.*
PSALM 126:5-6 NLT

◆

*"I have told you these things so that you will be*
*filled with my joy. Yes, your joy will overflow!"*
JOHN 15:11 NLT

*"God will let you laugh again;
you'll raise the roof with shouts of joy."*
JOB 8:21 MSG

◆

*But let all who take refuge in you rejoice; let them sing
joyful praises forever. Spread your protection over them,
that all who love your name may be filled with joy.*
PSALM 5:11 NLT

◆

*I will sing for joy in GOD, explode in praise from deep
in my soul! He dressed me up in a suit of salvation,
he outfitted me in a robe of righteousness, as a bridegroom
who puts on a tuxedo and a bride a jeweled tiara.*
ISAIAH 61:10 MSG

◆

*You will show me the way of life, granting me the joy of your
presence and the pleasures of living with you forever.*
PSALM 16:11 NLT

◆

*"But now I come to You, and these things I speak in the world,
that they may have My joy fulfilled in themselves."*
JOHN 17:13 NKJV

*Rejoice in the Lord always.*
*Again I will say, rejoice!*
PHILIPPIANS 4:4 NKJV

◆

*In the same way GOD's ransomed will come back,*
*come back to Zion cheering, shouting, joy eternal*
*wreathing their heads, exuberant ecstasies transporting*
*them—and not a sign of moans or groans.*
ISAIAH 51:11 MSG

◆

*A cheerful heart is good medicine,*
*but a crushed spirit dries up the bones.*
PROVERBS 17:22 NIV

◆

*But rejoice inasmuch as you participate in*
*the sufferings of Christ, so that you may be*
*overjoyed when his glory is revealed.*
1 PETER 4:13 NIV

◆

*Consider it a sheer gift, friends, when tests and challenges*
*come at you from all sides. You know that under pressure,*
*your faith-life is forced into the open and shows its true colors.*
JAMES 1:2–3 MSG

# Real Justice

*Share each other's burdens,*
*and in this way obey the law of Christ.*
GALATIANS 6:2 NLT

E mily had recently taken a greater interest in social justice issues and now was feeling overwhelmed. Hunger, poverty, war. . .the more she read and became aware about what was going on in the world, the more depressed and sad she became. She desperately wanted to help everyone who needed it, but nothing she did seemed to even make a dent in this enormous problem.

Many people today look at the seemingly dismal conditions of our world and become paralyzed by the enormity of it all. Some become so intimidated they end up doing nothing at all. It's important to remember that it's not our responsibility to solve the whole world's problems. Instead of becoming overwhelmed to the point of paralysis, we can be far more productive when we simply focus our energies on the people God brings across our paths each day.

Look around you. What needs do the people in your life have? Perhaps there's a local food pantry or homeless shelter where you can volunteer. Maybe there's a person on the subway or bus you ride that could use a listening ear. Making a small difference in the life of one person may not change the world, but it can make all the difference in the world to that one person.

*The good-hearted understand what it's like to be poor;*
*the hardhearted haven't the faintest idea.*
PROVERBS 29:7 MSG

*"Say no to wrong. Learn to do good. Work for justice.*
*Help the down-and-out. Stand up for the homeless.*
*Go to bat for the defenseless."*
ISAIAH 1:17 MSG

*The LORD is a shelter for the oppressed, a refuge in times of*
*trouble. Those who know your name trust in you, for you,*
*O LORD, do not abandon those who search for you.*
PSALM 9:9–10 NLT

*But God will never forget the needy;*
*the hope of the afflicted will never perish.*
PSALM 9:18 NIV

*"Don't pervert justice. Don't show favoritism to either the*
*poor or the great. Judge on the basis of what is right."*
LEVITICUS 19:15 MSG

*"Stop judging by mere appearances,*
*but instead judge correctly."*
JOHN 7:24 NIV

*Do not pervert justice or show partiality. Do not accept a bribe, for a bribe blinds the eyes of the wise and twists the words of the innocent. Follow justice and justice alone, so that you may live and possess the land the LORD your God is giving you.*

DEUTERONOMY 16:19–20 NIV

◆

*He shall bring forth your righteousness as the light, and your justice as the noonday.*

PSALM 37:6 NKJV

◆

*God has called us to live holy lives, not impure lives. Therefore, anyone who refuses to live by these rules is not disobeying human teaching but is rejecting God, who gives his Holy Spirit to you.*

1 THESSALONIANS 4:7–8 NLT

◆

*This is what the LORD says: Be fair-minded and just. Do what is right! Help those who have been robbed; rescue them from their oppressors. Quit your evil deeds! Do not mistreat foreigners, orphans, and widows. Stop murdering the innocent!*

JEREMIAH 22:3 NLT

◆

*"Thus says the LORD of hosts: 'Execute true justice, show mercy and compassion everyone to his brother.'"*

ZECHARIAH 7:9 NKJV

*This is what the Lord says: "Be just and fair to all.*
*Do what is right and good, for I am coming soon to rescue*
*you and to display my righteousness among you."*

ISAIAH 56:1 NLT

*Hate evil, love good; establish justice in the gate.*
*It may be that the Lord God of hosts will be gracious.*

AMOS 5:15 NKJV

*Good people celebrate when justice triumphs,*
*but for the workers of evil it's a bad day.*

PROVERBS 21:15 MSG

*Yet the Lord longs to be gracious to you; therefore he*
*will rise up to show you compassion. For the Lord is*
*a God of justice. Blessed are all who wait for him!*

ISAIAH 30:18 NIV

*He has shown you, O man, what is good; and what*
*does the Lord require of you but to do justly,*
*to love mercy, and to walk humbly with your God?*

MICAH 6:8 NKJV

# Good Fruit (of the Spirit)

*But the fruit of the Spirit is love, joy, peace, forbearance,*
*kindness, goodness, faithfulness, gentleness and*
*self-control. Against such things there is no law.*
GALATIANS 5:22–23 NIV

Have you ever watched apple trees produce apples? It's not exactly exciting. If they receive proper tending and get enough sunlight, water, and nourishment, they bear delicious fruit—no noticeable effort required.

Scripture often uses fruit analogies: we bear the fruit of the Spirit; Jesus prunes branches that don't bear fruit; we recognize other believers by the fruit their lives produce.

Sometimes we incorrectly think that fruit bearing is a goal that we're supposed to achieve—that productive Christians are required to work hard at doing and saying all the right things at all the right times. But working at being patient or kind simply doesn't work.

If you're feeling like you haven't been bearing much fruit lately, take a look at the environment you're planted in. Are you being regularly watered by God's Word? Are you basking in the sunlight of fellowship with other Christians? Are you being routinely nourished by prayer? If these things are a part of your life, soon you'll discover that the fruit you bear is the natural extension of God's love in you.

*The mind governed by the flesh is death, but the
mind governed by the Spirit is life and peace.*

ROMANS 8:6 NIV

◆

*If then you were raised with Christ, seek those things which
are above, where Christ is, sitting at the right hand of God.
Set your mind on things above, not on things on the earth.*

COLOSSIANS 3:1–2 NKJV

◆

*Then Abraham waited patiently,
and he received what God had promised.*

HEBREWS 6:15 NLT

◆

*Be humble and gentle. Be patient with each other, making
allowance for each other's faults because of your love.*

EPHESIANS 4:2 NLT

◆

*For you know that when your faith is tested,
your endurance has a chance to grow. So let it grow,
for when your endurance is fully developed, you will
be perfect and complete, needing nothing.*

JAMES 1:3–4 NLT

*"God is Spirit, and those who worship*
*Him must worship in spirit and truth."*
JOHN 4:24 NKJV

◆

*But you are not in the flesh but in the Spirit, if indeed*
*the Spirit of God dwells in you. Now if anyone does*
*not have the Spirit of Christ, he is not His.*
ROMANS 8:9 NKJV

◆

*And now I want each of you to extend that same intensity*
*toward a full-bodied hope, and keep at it till the finish.*
*Don't drag your feet. Be like those who stay the course with*
*committed faith and then get everything promised to them.*
HEBREWS 6:12 MSG

◆

*This calls for patient endurance on the part of the people of*
*God who keep his commands and remain faithful to Jesus.*
REVELATION 14:12 NIV

◆

*Make every effort to keep yourselves united in the Spirit,*
*binding yourselves together with peace.*
EPHESIANS 4:3 NLT

*I have been crucified with Christ; it is no longer I who live, but Christ lives in me; and the life which I now live in the flesh I live by faith in the Son of God, who loved me and gave Himself for me.*

GALATIANS 2:20 NKJV

◆

*"For it will not be you speaking, but the Spirit of your Father speaking through you."*

MATTHEW 10:20 NIV

◆

*Oh! May the God of green hope fill you up with joy, fill you up with peace, so that your believing lives, filled with the life-giving energy of the Holy Spirit, will brim over with hope!*

ROMANS 15:13 MSG

◆

*For the one whom God has sent speaks the words of God, for God gives the Spirit without limit.*

JOHN 3:34 NIV

◆

*And this hope will not lead to disappointment. For we know how dearly God loves us, because he has given us the Holy Spirit to fill our hearts with his love.*

ROMANS 5:5 NLT

# He Deserves My Praise: Worship

'One of the girls I go to school with does not have a great
voice, but every time she opens her mouth to sing, she pours
out her heart to God in worship. It made me realize that it
does not matter what I look like or sound like when I am
worshipping. As long as I am doing it with all my heart,
God will see it as a joyful noise unto Him. I should not be
worried about what others think of me and my worship style.

ELLEN WORSHAM, 19

The Bible says if we do not worship the Lord, the rocks
will cry out. Can you imagine rocks having to do the
work of God's people?

So what do we do? We worship the one true God, who
deserves our praise. And what does worship look like? It
can be as quiet as a head bowed in silent prayer and as
magnificent as a thousand-person choir lifting up its voice.
Worship has very few limits besides its focus. The *focus* of
our worship should always be the King.

Make your life an act of worship. Speak the name of
Jesus daily. Shine His light into a dark world. Sing your
heart out. Dance before Him. Play an instrument. Whisper
thanksgiving. Even rest can be an act of worship. God longs
for you to rest in His presence rather than rush through life
and miss Him.

How do you worship? Examine your personality,

style, talents, and personal relationship with Jesus. These will come together in a manner that fits who you are and proclaims who He is.

Praise the Lord, all His people! Praise Him in a million different ways. Praise Him with the powerful words of traditional hymns in your Sunday best. Praise Him in blue jeans at church on Saturday night. Worship Him with offerings of tithes, time, or talents. Be creative in your praise. And before you judge another's worship style, consider God's perspective. If someone worships Him with banners or tambourines, is that okay? If another chooses to light a candle or kneel down before Him, would you stop them? Will God receive their gift of worship? Certainly! Our God is not a stuffy ruler who has strict guidelines regarding worship. He takes great joy in any form of worship you give.

It is not nearly as important *how* you worship as it is that you simply *worship*. One day we will stand before Him in heaven and we will worship Him together with every instrument and song, every prayer, dance, and hymn! We will bow and dance and pray and sing and shout before King Jesus! Get started now. Live an abundant life of worship on this earth. This is just prep school for heaven!

*Praise the LORD. Praise God in his sanctuary;*
*praise him in his mighty heavens. Praise him for his*
*acts of power; praise him for his surpassing greatness.*
PSALM 150:1–2 NIV

◆

Christians come from all sorts of cultural backgrounds
and differ in worship style preferences. Make a conscious
decision not to judge those who worship differently from
you. There is not just one "right way" to praise our God.

◆

*Let everything that has breath praise the LORD.*
*Praise the LORD.*
PSALM 150:6 NIV

◆

At school I discovered that I can worship my Lord in many
other ways than just singing at church. Drawing, painting
in my journals, coffee dates encouraging sisters in Christ,
and using the gift of dance are just some of the many
ways He has given me to worship Him.
MOLLY WEISGARBER, 22

*Therefore I urge you, brethren, by the mercies of God,*
*to present your bodies a living and holy sacrifice,*
*acceptable to God, which is your spiritual service of worship.*
ROMANS 12:1 NASB

◆

Some of the very best worship happens when you become
still before God and simply rest in the peace that only
comes through Him. Express your heart to Him.
Tell Him how much He means to you.

◆

*The trumpeters and musicians joined in unison to give praise*
*and thanks to the LORD. Accompanied by trumpets, cymbals*
*and other instruments, the singers raised their voices in*
*praise to the LORD and sang: "He is good; his love endures*
*forever." Then the temple of the LORD was filled with the cloud.*
2 CHRONICLES 5:13 NIV

◆

Listen to praise and worship music. Wake up to it. Go to
sleep to it. Sing along. Close your eyes. Listen. Dwell
upon the offering of praise through melodies and words.
Weep. Feel. Rest. God loves it when you worship Him.

*"You must worship no other gods, for the Lord, whose very name is Jealous, is a God who is jealous about his relationship with you."*

EXODUS 34:14 NLT

◆

*Praise him with the sounding of the trumpet,
praise him with the harp and lyre,
praise him with timbrel and dancing,
praise him with the strings and pipe,
praise him with the clash of cymbals,
praise him with resounding cymbals.*

PSALM 150:3–5 NIV

◆

Ask God to give you a hunger and thirst for worship that you might become a believer who is always entering into His presence to give Him praise, regardless of your circumstances.

◆

*Jesus said to him, "Away from me, Satan! For it is written: 'Worship the Lord your God, and serve him only.'"*

MATTHEW 4:10 NIV

◆

The simplest act can be an act of worship. A gift given in the name of Jesus is worship. A smile, a kind word spoken, a head bowed before a meal, and even silence are forms of worship.

# CHOOSE PRAISE

*Because your love is better than life, my lips will*
*glorify you. I will praise you as long as I live,*
*and in your name I will lift up my hands.*

PSALM 63:3–4 NIV

Kendra's father was one of her best friends. They often worked side by side—putting up Christmas lights, planting flowers in the garden, or puttering in the basement. When her father suffered a stroke at age fifty-seven, Kendra was shocked. Her heart broke to see him confined to a hospital bed, struggling to remember familiar names and complete simple tasks. Kendra began slipping into feelings of depression, until something her mother said changed everything.

"Even though I don't understand why this happened," her mother said through tears, "instead of asking why, I *choose* to praise."

It's natural to praise God when life is going our way. We are thankful, joyful, obedient—God has blessed us! But when faced with difficult circumstances, when our questions remain unanswered, it is easy to become hopeless and depressed.

No matter what life brings, it is important to remember that we always have a choice. We can choose to resign ourselves to defeat, becoming bitter and miserable; or we can praise the One who knows best, who loves us the very most. Praising God doesn't change our circumstances, but it does change our hearts. And that changes everything.

*Oh come, let us worship and bow down;*
*let us kneel before the LORD our Maker.*

◆

Do not wait until Sunday when you "go to worship."
Worship every day. Worship in your car on the way to work.
Worship in quiet meditation and through song and dance.
Worship does not require a praise band or a pipe organ.
It can happen anywhere, anytime. Praise the Lord.

◆

*For what you have done I will always praise you*
*in the presence of your faithful people. And I will*
*hope in your name, for your name is good.*

PSALM 52:9 NIV

◆

*"The LORD is my strength and song, and He has become my*
*salvation; He is my God, and I will praise Him;*
*my father's God, and I will exalt Him."*

EXODUS 15:2 NKJV

◆

*All the nations you made will come and bow before you,*
*Lord; they will praise your holy name.*

PSALM 86:9 NLT

*Give to the LORD the glory he deserves!*
*Bring your offering and come into his presence.*
*Worship the LORD in all his holy splendor.*
1 CHRONICLES 16:29 NLT

◆

*"My soul magnifies the Lord."*
LUKE 1:46 NKJV

◆

*I will proclaim the name of the LORD.*
*Oh, praise the greatness of our God!*
DEUTERONOMY 32:3 NIV

◆

*Break forth into joy, sing together. . . .*
*For the LORD has comforted His people.*
ISAIAH 52:9 NKJV

◆

*Worship the LORD with gladness.*
*Come before him, singing with joy.*
PSALM 100:2 NLT

◆

*"The LORD lives! Praise be to my Rock!*
*Exalted be my God, the Rock, my Savior!"*
2 SAMUEL 22:47 NIV

*Therefore by Him let us continually offer the
sacrifice of praise to God, that is, the fruit
of our lips, giving thanks to His name.*
HEBREWS 13:15 NKJV

◆

*For great is his love toward us, and the faithfulness
of the LORD endures forever. Praise the LORD.*
PSALM 117:2 NIV

◆

*To all who mourn in Israel, he will give a crown of beauty for
ashes, a joyous blessing instead of mourning, festive praise
instead of despair. In their righteousness, they will be like
great oaks that the LORD has planted for his own glory.*
ISAIAH 61:3 NLT

◆

*How blessed is God! And what a blessing he is!
He's the Father of our Master, Jesus Christ,
and takes us to the high places of blessing in him.*
EPHESIANS 1:3 MSG

◆

*And here we are, O God, our God,
giving thanks to you, praising your splendid Name.*
1 CHRONICLES 29:13 MSG

# Into the Unknown: My Future

A verse that has always brought peace and confidence when I begin to worry about future decisions is Philippians 1:6 (NIV): "[Be] confident of this, that he who began a good work in you will carry it on to completion until the day of Christ Jesus."

MOLLY WEISGARBER, 22

S etting out on a long road trip without a map or GPS would be a bit unsettling, particularly to people who do not like to stop and ask for directions. But the truth is, life on earth is a journey with little direction! There was no map sent home with you from the hospital at birth that plotted out the roads you should travel through your school years and into adulthood. A lot of it may seem like guesswork, but not for the Christian. God has given us a guidebook called the Bible. He has offered us a Guide to direct us in His wise and loving Holy Spirit. His commands provide an outline. Through prayer and fellowship with Him, the Lord fills in the gaps so that we might know where to go and what to do along the way.

Even so, facing an uncertain future can be frightening. We have to submit our weakness and our fear to God, trusting Him to take care of us one day at a time. He will never reveal to us more than we need to know in the moment. His children have to trust in the dark what He has proven to them in the light. He is faithful; He cannot be anything less.

Base your trust in Him for your future on what God has shown.you in the past.

In Bible times, God's chosen people would build an altar at the spot where God showed Himself faithful. The altar served as a reminder for them and for their children that the Lord of the universe had provided and would continue to provide for them. Build some altars in your own life. When God proves Himself faithful to you, write it down. Mark the date and the answer to prayer or the miracle that He gave to you. As you face uncertain times and step into a future that you cannot predict, you will do so with greater peace if you can reflect on the milestones of God's faithfulness.

The Bible points out that if human parents know how to give good gifts to their children, then, of course, our heavenly Father knows what we need and how to bless us! God is out for your best interest. Nothing will happen to you in the present or in the future that has not first been filtered through His fingers. Rest in that, and face the future with joy in your heart.

*Oh, Father, I long for the day we will sing and praise Your name together in heaven. Until then, let us accept that there are various ways to worship. Unify us as we praise You, each in our own way. Amen.*

*For I am convinced that neither death nor life, neither*
*angels nor demons, neither the present nor the future,*
*nor any powers, neither height nor depth, nor anything*
*else in all creation, will be able to separate us from*
*the love of God that is in Christ Jesus our Lord.*

ROMANS 8:38–39 NIV

*Give all your worries and cares to God,*
*for he cares about you.*

1 PETER 5:7 NLT

*"For I know the plans I have for you," declares the LORD,*
*"plans to prosper you and not to harm you,*
*plans to give you hope and a future."*

JEREMIAH 29:11 NIV

Each new day, submit your steps to Jesus. Ask that He reveal to you what you need to know for that day and give you the strength to honor Him in all things. If you take it one day at a time, the future will seem much less daunting.

*"So don't worry about these things, saying, 'What will
we eat? What will we drink? What will we wear?'
These things dominate the thoughts of unbelievers,
but your heavenly Father already knows all your needs.
Seek the Kingdom of God above all else, and live
righteously, and he will give you everything you need."*
MATTHEW 6:31–33 NLT

◆

*The blameless spend their days under the LORD's care,
and their inheritance will endure forever. In times
of disaster they will not wither; in days of famine
they will enjoy plenty. But the wicked will perish.*
PSALM 37:18–20 NIV

◆

If fear of the future had overtaken them, Ruth would
have left Naomi alone, Noah would never have built the
ark, and Daniel certainly would have bowed to King
Nebuchadnezzar. Trust the Lord in the same way that
believers who came before you trusted Him with the future.

◆

*LORD, I know that people's lives are not their own;
it is not for them to direct their steps.*
JEREMIAH 10:23 NIV

*"Therefore do not worry about tomorrow, for tomorrow will
worry about itself. Each day has enough trouble of its own."*
MATTHEW 6:34 NIV

I underestimated the value of long-term goals when I was in
college. I knew they were important, but the actual reality
of their importance was diminished by my instructors' and
advisers' assurances that I could do whatever I wanted, take
my time figuring it out, and that I didn't have to decide right
away. But when you follow that kind of advice, it leads to so
much anxiety and uncertainty. I think a better way to go
about planning for the future is to have several long-term
goals or life scenarios in mind that you'd like to achieve.
Committing yourself to a clear direction and knowing what's
really going to make you happy makes a huge difference.

ASHLEY CASTEEL, 23

*All the days ordained for me were written
in your book before one of them came to be.*
PSALM 139:16 NIV

The same God who has held the world together in the past holds it in the palm of His hand today. Until He determines otherwise, the sun will rise and set each new day. When Jesus returns, He will gather His own unto Himself and take us up into heaven with Him. Wow, what a future we have to look forward to!

◆

*The LORD will vindicate me; your love, LORD, endures forever—
do not abandon the works of your hands.*

PSALM 138:8 NIV

◆

Have you considered that it actually insults God when you worry about your future? He has promised you that He will take care of it. Would you want someone to question you again and again about a promise you had made? Instead, would you not want that person to trust you?

# MAKING GOOD DECISIONS

*"Choose my instruction instead of silver, knowledge rather
than choice gold, for wisdom is more precious than rubies,
and nothing you desire can compare with her."*

PROVERBS 8:10–11 NIV

◆

A nn felt as if she were about to take the bungee jump
of her life—blindfolded. Quitting her secure and well-
paying job to pursue her dream of going back to school
to become a teacher seemed like the right thing to do, but
doubt nagged her.

*What if I can't make it financially? What if going back
to school is harder than I thought? What if teaching isn't for
me?* Despite Ann's questions, her heart wouldn't let go of
the dream of opening a tutoring center for underprivileged
children.

One morning, after a sleepless night of praying for
wisdom, the answers seemed clear. She wasn't jumping
blindly. She had carefully researched her options. She'd
asked for advice from trusted friends. And most importantly,
she believed God had prompted her to make this decision.

God's wisdom helps us make good decisions and keeps
us from dangerous situations. But sometimes this wisdom
seems so difficult to find. How do we really *know* when
our plans for the future are part of God's plan? The key is
consistency—faithfully seeking God's will, through His Word
and through prayer; asking others for advice. Gradually
the wise choice becomes clear. God imparts wisdom for the
future. It's ours for the asking.

*Talk to Wisdom as to a sister.*
*Treat Insight as your companion.*
PROVERBS 7:4 MSG

*In that day he will be your sure foundation,*
*providing a rich store of salvation, wisdom, and*
*knowledge. The fear of the LORD will be your treasure.*
ISAIAH 33:6 NLT

*For your obedience has become known to all.*
*Therefore I am glad on your behalf; but I want you to*
*be wise in what is good, and simple concerning evil.*
ROMANS 16:19 NKJV

*"Those who are wise will shine like the brightness*
*of the heavens, and those who lead many to*
*righteousness; like the stars for ever and ever."*
DANIEL 12:3 NIV

*Whoever obeys his command will come to no harm,*
*and the wise heart will know the proper time and procedure.*
ECCLESIASTES 8:5 NIV

*"Therefore everyone who hears these words of mine and puts them into practice is like a wise man who built his house on the rock. The rain came down, the streams rose, and the winds blew and beat against that house; yet it did not fall, because it had its foundation on the rock."*

MATTHEW 7:24–25 NIV

◆

*If you are really wise, you'll think this over—
it's time you appreciated GOD's deep love.*

PSALM 107:43 MSG

◆

*Who is wise and understanding among you?
Let him show by good conduct that his works
are done in the meekness of wisdom.*

JAMES 3:13 NKJV

◆

*We declare God's wisdom, a mystery that has been hidden
and that God destined for our glory before time began.*

1 CORINTHIANS 2:7 NIV

◆

*How much better to get wisdom than gold! And to get
understanding is to be chosen rather than silver.*

PROVERBS 16:16 NKJV

# Read Thru the Bible in a Year

| | | | |
|---|---|---|---|
| 1-Jan | Gen. 1-2 | Matt. 1 | Ps. 1 |
| 2-Jan | Gen. 3-4 | Matt. 2 | Ps. 2 |
| 3-Jan | Gen. 5-7 | Matt. 3 | Ps. 3 |
| 4-Jan | Gen. 8-10 | Matt. 4 | Ps. 4 |
| 5-Jan | Gen. 11-13 | Matt. 5:1-20 | Ps. 5 |
| 6-Jan | Gen. 14-16 | Matt. 5:21-48 | Ps. 6 |
| 7-Jan | Gen. 17-18 | Matt. 6:1-18 | Ps. 7 |
| 8-Jan | Gen. 19-20 | Matt. 6:19-34 | Ps. 8 |
| 9-Jan | Gen. 21-23 | Matt. 7:1-11 | Ps. 9:1-8 |
| 10-Jan | Gen. 24 | Matt. 7:12-29 | Ps. 9:9-20 |
| 11-Jan | Gen. 25-26 | Matt. 8:1-17 | Ps. 10:1-11 |
| 12-Jan | Gen. 27:1-28:9 | Matt. 8:18-34 | Ps. 10:12-18 |
| 13-Jan | Gen. 28:10-29:35 | Matt. 9 | Ps. 11 |
| 14-Jan | Gen. 30:1-31:21 | Matt. 10:1-15 | Ps. 12 |
| 15-Jan | Gen. 31:22-32:21 | Matt. 10:16-36 | Ps. 13 |
| 16-Jan | Gen. 32:22-34:31 | Matt. 10:37-11:6 | Ps. 14 |
| 17-Jan | Gen. 35-36 | Matt. 11:7-24 | Ps. 15 |
| 18-Jan | Gen. 37-38 | Matt. 11:25-30 | Ps. 16 |
| 19-Jan | Gen. 39-40 | Matt. 12:1-29 | Ps. 17 |
| 20-Jan | Gen. 41 | Matt. 12:30-50 | Ps. 18:1-15 |
| 21-Jan | Gen. 42-43 | Matt. 13:1-9 | Ps. 18:16-29 |
| 22-Jan | Gen. 44-45 | Matt. 13:10-23 | Ps. 18:30-50 |
| 23-Jan | Gen. 46:1-47:26 | Matt. 13:24-43 | Ps. 19 |
| 24-Jan | Gen. 47:27-49:28 | Matt. 13:44-58 | Ps. 20 |
| 25-Jan | Gen. 49:29-Exod. 1:22 | Matt. 14 | Ps. 21 |
| 26-Jan | Exod. 2-3 | Matt. 15:1-28 | Ps. 22:1-21 |
| 27-Jan | Exod. 4:1-5:21 | Matt. 15:29-16:12 | Ps. 22:22-31 |
| 28-Jan | Exod. 5:22-7:24 | Matt. 16:13-28 | Ps. 23 |
| 29-Jan | Exod. 7:25-9:35 | Matt. 17:1-9 | Ps. 24 |
| 30-Jan | Exod. 10-11 | Matt. 17:10-27 | Ps. 25 |
| 31-Jan | Exod. 12 | Matt. 18:1-20 | Ps. 26 |
| 1-Feb | Exod. 13-14 | Matt. 18:21-35 | Ps. 27 |
| 2-Feb | Exod. 15-16 | Matt. 19:1-15 | Ps. 28 |
| 3-Feb | Exod. 17-19 | Matt. 19:16-30 | Ps. 29 |
| 4-Feb | Exod. 20-21 | Matt. 20:1-19 | Ps. 30 |
| 5-Feb | Exod. 22-23 | Matt. 20:20-34 | Ps. 31:1-8 |
| 6-Feb | Exod. 24-25 | Matt. 21:1-27 | Ps. 31:9-18 |
| 7-Feb | Exod 26-27 | Matt. 21:28-46 | Ps. 31:19-24 |
| 8-Feb | Exod. 28 | Matt. 22 | Ps. 32 |
| 9-Feb | Exod. 29 | Matt. 23:1-36 | Ps. 33:1-12 |
| 10-Feb | Exod. 30-31 | Matt. 23:37-24:28 | Ps. 33:13-22 |
| 11-Feb | Exod. 32-33 | Matt. 24:29-51 | Ps. 34:1-7 |
| 12-Feb | Exod. 34:1-35:29 | Matt. 25:1-13 | Ps. 34:8-22 |
| 13-Feb | Exod. 35:30-37:29 | Matt. 25:14-30 | Ps. 35:1-8 |
| 14-Feb | Exod. 38-39 | Matt. 25:31-46 | Ps. 35:9-17 |
| 15-Feb | Exod. 40 | Matt. 26:1-35 | Ps. 35:18-28 |
| 16-Feb | Lev. 1-3 | Matt. 26:36-68 | Ps. 36:1-6 |
| 17-Feb | Lev. 4:1-5:13 | Matt. 26:69-27:26 | Ps. 36:7-12 |
| 18-Feb | Lev. 5:14-7:21 | Matt. 27:27-50 | Ps. 37:1-6 |

| | | | |
|---|---|---|---|
| 19-Feb | Lev. 7:22-8:36 | Matt. 27:51-66 | Ps. 37:7-26 |
| 20-Feb | Lev. 9-10 | Matt. 28 | Ps. 37:27-40 |
| 21-Feb | Lev. 11-12 | Mark 1:1-28 | Ps. 38 |
| 22-Feb | Lev. 13 | Mark 1:29-39 | Ps. 39 |
| 23-Feb | Lev. 14 | Mark 1:40-2:12 | Ps. 40:1-8 |
| 24-Feb | Lev. 15 | Mark 2:13-3:35 | Ps. 40:9-17 |
| 25-Feb | Lev. 16-17 | Mark 4:1-20 | Ps. 41:1-4 |
| 26-Feb | Lev. 18-19 | Mark 4:21-41 | Ps. 41:5-13 |
| 27-Feb | Lev. 20 | Mark 5 | Ps. 42-43 |
| 28-Feb | Lev. 21-22 | Mark 6:1-13 | Ps. 44 |
| 1-Mar | Lev. 23-24 | Mark 6:14-29 | Ps. 45:1-5 |
| 2-Mar | Lev. 25 | Mark 6:30-56 | Ps. 45:6-12 |
| 3-Mar | Lev. 26 | Mark 7 | Ps. 45:13-17 |
| 4-Mar | Lev. 27 | Mark 8 | Ps. 46 |
| 5-Mar | Num. 1-2 | Mark 9:1-13 | Ps. 47 |
| 6-Mar | Num. 3 | Mark 9:14-50 | Ps. 48:1-8 |
| 7-Mar | Num. 4 | Mark 10:1-34 | Ps. 48:9-14 |
| 8-Mar | Num. 5:1-6:21 | Mark 10:35-52 | Ps. 49:1-9 |
| 9-Mar | Num. 6:22-7:47 | Mark 11 | Ps. 49:10-20 |
| 10-Mar | Num. 7:48-8:4 | Mark 12:1-27 | Ps. 50:1-15 |
| 11-Mar | Num. 8:5-9:23 | Mark 12:28-44 | Ps. 50:16-23 |
| 12-Mar | Num. 10-11 | Mark 13:1-8 | Ps. 51:1-9 |
| 13-Mar | Num. 12-13 | Mark 13:9-37 | Ps. 51:10-19 |
| 14-Mar | Num. 14 | Mark 14:1-31 | Ps. 52 |
| 15-Mar | Num. 15 | Mark 14:32-72 | Ps. 53 |
| 16-Mar | Num. 16 | Mark 15:1-32 | Ps. 54 |
| 17-Mar | Num. 17-18 | Mark 15:33-47 | Ps. 55 |
| 18-Mar | Num. 19-20 | Mark 16 | Ps. 56:1-7 |
| 19-Mar | Num. 21:1-22:20 | Luke 1:1-25 | Ps. 56:8-13 |
| 20-Mar | Num. 22:21-23:30 | Luke 1:26-56 | Ps. 57 |
| 21-Mar | Num. 24-25 | Luke 1:57-2:20 | Ps. 58 |
| 22-Mar | Num. 26:1-27:11 | Luke 2:21-38 | Ps. 59:1-8 |
| 23-Mar | Num. 27:12-29:11 | Luke 2:39-52 | Ps. 59:9-17 |
| 24-Mar | Num. 29:12-30:16 | Luke 3 | Ps. 60:1-5 |
| 25-Mar | Num. 31 | Luke 4 | Ps. 60:6-12 |
| 26-Mar | Num. 32-33 | Luke 5:1-16 | Ps. 61 |
| 27-Mar | Num. 34-36 | Luke 5:17-32 | Ps. 62:1-6 |
| 28-Mar | Deut. 1:1-2:25 | Luke 5:33-6:11 | Ps. 62:7-12 |
| 29-Mar | Deut. 2:26-4:14 | Luke 6:12-35 | Ps. 63:1-5 |
| 30-Mar | Deut. 4:15-5:22 | Luke 6:36-49 | Ps. 63:6-11 |
| 31-Mar | Deut. 5:23-7:26 | Luke 7:1-17 | Ps. 64:1-5 |
| 1-Apr | Deut. 8-9 | Luke 7:18-35 | Ps. 64:6-10 |
| 2-Apr | Deut. 10-11 | Luke 7:36-8:3 | Ps. 65:1-8 |
| 3-Apr | Deut. 12-13 | Luke 8:4-21 | Ps. 65:9-13 |
| 4-Apr | Deut. 14:1-16:8 | Luke 8:22-39 | Ps. 66:1-7 |
| 5-Apr | Deut. 16:9-18:22 | Luke 8:40-56 | Ps. 66:8-15 |
| 6-Apr | Deut. 19:1-21:9 | Luke 9:1-22 | Ps. 66:16-20 |
| 7-Apr | Deut. 21:10-23:8 | Luke 9:23-42 | Ps. 67 |
| 8-Apr | Deut. 23:9-25:19 | Luke 9:43-62 | Ps. 68:1-6 |
| 9-Apr | Deut. 26:1-28:14 | Luke 10:1-20 | Ps. 68:7-14 |
| 10-Apr | Deut. 28:15-68 | Luke 10:21-37 | Ps. 68:15-19 |
| 11-Apr | Deut. 29-30 | Luke 10:38-11:23 | Ps. 68:20-27 |
| 12-Apr | Deut. 31:1-32:22 | Luke 11:24-36 | Ps. 68:28-35 |
| 13-Apr | Deut. 32:23-33:29 | Luke 11:37-54 | Ps. 69:1-9 |

| | | | |
|---|---|---|---|
| 14-Apr | Deut. 34-Josh. 2 | Luke 12:1-15 | Ps. 69:10-17 |
| 15-Apr | Josh. 3:1-5:12 | Luke 12:16-40 | Ps. 69:18-28 |
| 16-Apr | Josh. 5:13-7:26 | Luke 12:41-48 | Ps. 69:29-36 |
| 17-Apr | Josh. 8-9 | Luke 12:49-59 | Ps. 70 |
| 18-Apr | Josh. 10:1-11:15 | Luke 13:1-21 | Ps. 71:1-6 |
| 19-Apr | Josh. 11:16-13:33 | Luke 13:22-35 | Ps. 71:7-16 |
| 20-Apr | Josh. 14-16 | Luke 14:1-15 | Ps. 71:17-21 |
| 21-Apr | Josh. 17:1-19:16 | Luke 14:16-35 | Ps. 71:22-24 |
| 22-Apr | Josh. 19:17-21:42 | Luke 15:1-10 | Ps. 72:1-11 |
| 23-Apr | Josh. 21:43-22:34 | Luke 15:11-32 | Ps. 72:12-20 |
| 24-Apr | Josh. 23-24 | Luke 16:1-18 | Ps. 73:1-9 |
| 25-Apr | Judg. 1-2 | Luke 16:19-17:10 | Ps. 73:10-20 |
| 26-Apr | Judg. 3-4 | Luke 17:11-37 | Ps. 73:21-28 |
| 27-Apr | Judg. 5:1-6:24 | Luke 18:1-17 | Ps. 74:1-3 |
| 28-Apr | Judg. 6:25-7:25 | Luke 18:18-43 | Ps. 74:4-11 |
| 29-Apr | Judg. 8:1-9:23 | Luke 19:1-28 | Ps. 74:12-17 |
| 30-Apr | Judg. 9:24-10:18 | Luke 19:29-48 | Ps. 74:18-23 |
| 1-May | Judg. 11:1-12:7 | Luke 20:1-26 | Ps. 75:1-7 |
| 2-May | Judg. 12:8-14:20 | Luke 20:27-47 | Ps. 75:8-10 |
| 3-May | Judg. 15-16 | Luke 21:1-19 | Ps. 76:1-7 |
| 4-May | Judg. 17-18 | Luke 21:20-22:6 | Ps. 76:8-12 |
| 5-May | Judg. 19:1-20:23 | Luke 22:7-30 | Ps. 77:1-11 |
| 6-May | Judg. 20:24-21:25 | Luke 22:31-54 | Ps. 77:12-20 |
| 7-May | Ruth 1-2 | Luke 22:55-23:25 | Ps. 78:1-4 |
| 8-May | Ruth 3-4 | Luke 23:26-24:12 | Ps. 78:5-8 |
| 9-May | 1 Sam. 1:1-2:21 | Luke 24:13-53 | Ps. 78:9-16 |
| 10-May | 1 Sam. 2:22-4:22 | John 1:1-28 | Ps. 78:17-24 |
| 11-May | 1 Sam. 5-7 | John 1:29-51 | Ps. 78:25-33 |
| 12-May | 1 Sam. 8:1-9:26 | John 2 | Ps. 78:34-41 |
| 13-May | 1 Sam. 9:27-11:15 | John 3:1-22 | Ps. 78:42-55 |
| 14-May | 1 Sam. 12-13 | John 3:23-4:10 | Ps. 78:56-66 |
| 15-May | 1 Sam. 14 | John 4:11-38 | Ps. 78:67-72 |
| 16-May | 1 Sam. 15-16 | John 4:39-54 | Ps. 79:1-7 |
| 17-May | 1 Sam. 17 | John 5:1-24 | Ps. 79:8-13 |
| 18-May | 1 Sam. 18-19 | John 5:25-47 | Ps. 80:1-7 |
| 19-May | 1 Sam. 20-21 | John 6:1-21 | Ps. 80:8-19 |
| 20-May | 1 Sam. 22-23 | John 6:22-42 | Ps. 81:1-10 |
| 21-May | 1 Sam. 24:1-25:31 | John 6:43-71 | Ps. 81:11-16 |
| 22-May | 1 Sam. 25:32-27:12 | John 7:1-24 | Ps. 82 |
| 23-May | 1 Sam. 28-29 | John 7:25-8:11 | Ps. 83 |
| 24-May | 1 Sam. 30-31 | John 8:12-47 | Ps. 84:1-4 |
| 25-May | 2 Sam. 1-2 | John 8:48-9:12 | Ps. 84:5-12 |
| 26-May | 2 Sam. 3-4 | John 9:13-34 | Ps. 85:1-7 |
| 27-May | 2 Sam. 5:1-7:17 | John 9:35-10:10 | Ps. 85:8-13 |
| 28-May | 2 Sam. 7:18-10:19 | John 10:11-30 | Ps. 86:1-10 |
| 29-May | 2 Sam. 11:1-12:25 | John 10:31-11:16 | Ps. 86:11-17 |
| 30-May | 2 Sam. 12:26-13:39 | John 11:17-54 | Ps. 87 |
| 31-May | 2 Sam. 14:1-15:12 | John 11:55-12:19 | Ps. 88:1-9 |
| 1-Jun | 2 Sam. 15:13-16:23 | John 12:20-43 | Ps. 88:10-18 |
| 2-Jun | 2 Sam. 17:1-18:18 | John 12:44-13:20 | Ps. 89:1-6 |
| 3-Jun | 2 Sam. 18:19-19:39 | John 13:21-38 | Ps. 89:7-13 |
| 4-Jun | 2 Sam. 19:40-21:22 | John 14:1-17 | Ps. 89:14-18 |
| 5-Jun | 2 Sam. 22:1-23:7 | John 14:18-15:27 | Ps. 89:19-29 |
| 6-Jun | 2 Sam. 23:8-24:25 | John 16:1-22 | Ps. 89:30-37 |

| | | | |
|---|---|---|---|
| 7-Jun | 1 Kings 1 | John 16:23-17:5 | Ps. 89:38-52 |
| 8-Jun | 1 Kings 2 | John 17:6-26 | Ps. 90:1-12 |
| 9-Jun | 1 Kings 3-4 | John 18:1-27 | Ps. 90:13-17 |
| 10-Jun | 1 Kings 5-6 | John 18:28-19:5 | Ps. 91:1-10 |
| 11-Jun | 1 Kings 7 | John 19:6-25a | Ps. 91:11-16 |
| 12-Jun | 1 Kings 8:1-53 | John 19:25b-42 | Ps. 92:1-9 |
| 13-Jun | 1 Kings 8:54-10:13 | John 20:1-18 | Ps. 92:10-15 |
| 14-Jun | 1 Kings 10:14-11:43 | John 20:19-31 | Ps. 93 |
| 15-Jun | 1 Kings 12:1-13:10 | John 21 | Ps. 94:1-11 |
| 16-Jun | 1 Kings 13:11-14:31 | Acts 1:1-11 | Ps. 94:12-23 |
| 17-Jun | 1 Kings 15:1-16:20 | Acts 1:12-26 | Ps. 95 |
| 18-Jun | 1 Kings 16:21-18:19 | Acts 2:1-21 | Ps. 96:1-8 |
| 19-Jun | 1 Kings 18:20-19:21 | Acts2:22-41 | Ps. 96:9-13 |
| 20-Jun | 1 Kings 20 | Acts 2:42-3:26 | Ps. 97:1-6 |
| 21-Jun | 1 Kings 21:1-22:28 | Acts 4:1-22 | Ps. 97:7-12 |
| 22-Jun | 1 Kings 22:29- 2 Kings 1:18 | Acts 4:23-5:11 | Ps. 98 |
| 23-Jun | 2 Kings 2-3 | Acts 5:12-28 | Ps. 99 |
| 24-Jun | 2 Kings 4 | Acts 5:29-6:15 | Ps. 100 |
| 25-Jun | 2 Kings 5:1-6:23 | Acts 7:1-16 | Ps. 101 |
| 26-Jun | 2 Kings 6:24-8:15 | Acts 7:17-36 | Ps. 102:1-7 |
| 27-Jun | 2 Kings 8:16-9:37 | Acts 7:37-53 | Ps. 102:8-17 |
| 28-Jun | 2 Kings 10-11 | Acts 7:54-8:8 | Ps. 102:18-28 |
| 29-Jun | 2 Kings 12-13 | Acts 8:9-40 | Ps. 103:1-9 |
| 30-Jun | 2 Kings 14-15 | Acts 9:1-16 | Ps. 103:10-14 |
| 1-Jul | 2 Kings 16-17 | Acts 9:17-31 | Ps. 103:15-22 |
| 2-Jul | 2 Kings 18:1-19:7 | Acts 9:32-10:16 | Ps. 104:1-9 |
| 3-Jul | 2 Kings 19:8-20:21 | Acts 10:17-33 | Ps. 104:10-23 |
| 4-Jul | 2 Kings 21:1-22:20 | Acts 10:34-11:18 | Ps. 104: 24-30 |
| 5-Jul | 2 Kings 23 | Acts 11:19-12:17 | Ps. 104:31-35 |
| 6-Jul | 2 Kings 24-25 | Acts 12:18-13:13 | Ps. 105:1-7 |
| 7-Jul | 1 Chron. 1-2 | Acts 13:14-43 | Ps. 105:8-15 |
| 8-Jul | 1 Chron. 3:1-5:10 | Acts 13:44-14:10 | Ps. 105:16-28 |
| 9-Jul | 1 Chron. 5:11-6:81 | Acts 14:11-28 | Ps. 105:29-36 |
| 10-Jul | 1 Chron. 7:1-9:9 | Acts 15:1-18 | Ps. 105:37-45 |
| 11-Jul | 1 Chron. 9:10-11:9 | Acts 15:19-41 | Ps. 106:1-12 |
| 12-Jul | 1 Chron. 11:10-12:40 | Acts 16:1-15 | Ps. 106:13-27 |
| 13-Jul | 1 Chron. 13-15 | Acts 16:16-40 | Ps. 106:28-33 |
| 14-Jul | 1 Chron. 16-17 | Acts 17:1-14 | Ps. 106:34-43 |
| 15-Jul | 1 Chron. 18-20 | Acts 17:15-34 | Ps. 106:44-48 |
| 16-Jul | 1 Chron. 21-22 | Acts 18:1-23 | Ps. 107:1-9 |
| 17-Jul | 1 Chron. 23-25 | Acts 18:24-19:10 | Ps. 107:10-16 |
| 18-Jul | 1 Chron. 26-27 | Acts 19:11-22 | Ps. 107:17-32 |
| 19-Jul | 1 Chron. 28-29 | Acts 19:23-41 | Ps. 107:33-38 |
| 20-Jul | 2 Chron. 1-3 | Acts 20:1-16 | Ps. 107:39-43 |
| 21-Jul | 2 Chron. 4:1-6:11 | Acts 20:17-38 | Ps. 108 |
| 22-Jul | 2 Chron. 6:12-7:10 | Acts 21:1-14 | Ps. 109:1-20 |
| 23-Jul | 2 Chron. 7:11-9:28 | Acts 21:15-32 | Ps. 109:21-31 |
| 24-Jul | 2 Chron. 9:29-12:16 | Acts 21:33-22:16 | Ps. 110:1-3 |
| 25-Jul | 2 Chron. 13-15 | Acts 22:17-23:11 | Ps. 110:4-7 |
| 26-Jul | 2 Chron. 16-17 | Acts 23:12-24:21 | Ps. 111 |
| 27-Jul | 2 Chron. 18-19 | Acts 24:22-25:12 | Ps. 112 |
| 28-Jul | 2 Chron. 20-21 | Acts 25:13-27 | Ps. 113 |
| 29-Jul | 2 Chron. 22-23 | Acts 26 | Ps. 114 |

| | | | |
|---|---|---|---|
| 30-Jul | 2 Chron. 24:1-25:16 | Acts 27:1-20 | Ps. 115:1-10 |
| 31-Jul | 2 Chron. 25:17-27:9 | Acts 27:21-28:6 | Ps. 115:11-18 |
| 1-Aug | 2 Chron. 28:1-29:19 | Acts 28:7-31 | Ps. 116:1-5 |
| 2-Aug | 2 Chron. 29:20-30:27 | Rom. 1:1-17 | Ps. 116:6-19 |
| 3-Aug | 2 Chron. 31-32 | Rom. 1:18-32 | Ps. 117 |
| 4-Aug | 2 Chron. 33:1-34:7 | Rom. 2 | Ps. 118:1-18 |
| 5-Aug | 2 Chron. 34:8-35:19 | Rom. 3:1-26 | Ps. 118:19-23 |
| 6-Aug | 2 Chron. 35:20-36:23 | Rom. 3:27-4:25 | Ps. 118:24-29 |
| 7-Aug | Ezra 1-3 | Rom. 5 | Ps. 119:1-8 |
| 8-Aug | Ezra 4-5 | Rom. 6:1-7:6 | Ps. 119:9-16 |
| 9-Aug | Ezra 6:1-7:26 | Rom. 7:7-25 | Ps. 119:17-32 |
| 10-Aug | Ezra 7:27-9:4 | Rom. 8:1-27 | Ps. 119:33-40 |
| 11-Aug | Ezra 9:5-10:44 | Rom. 8:28-39 | Ps. 119:41-64 |
| 12-Aug | Neh. 1:1-3:16 | Rom. 9:1-18 | Ps. 119:65-72 |
| 13-Aug | Neh. 3:17-5:13 | Rom. 9:19-33 | Ps. 119:73-80 |
| 14-Aug | Neh. 5:14-7:73 | Rom. 10:1-13 | Ps. 119:81-88 |
| 15-Aug | Neh. 8:1-9:5 | Rom. 10:14-11:24 | Ps. 119:89-104 |
| 16-Aug | Neh. 9:6-10:27 | Rom. 11:25-12:8 | Ps. 119:105-120 |
| 17-Aug | Neh. 10:28-12:26 | Rom. 12:9-13:7 | Ps. 119:121-128 |
| 18-Aug | Neh. 12:27-13:31 | Rom. 13:8-14:12 | Ps. 119:129-136 |
| 19-Aug | Esther 1:1-2:18 | Rom. 14:13-15:13 | Ps. 119:137-152 |
| 20-Aug | Esther 2:19-5:14 | Rom. 15:14-21 | Ps. 119:153-168 |
| 21-Aug | Esther. 6-8 | Rom. 15:22-33 | Ps. 119:169-176 |
| 22-Aug | Esther 9-10 | Rom. 16 | Ps. 120-122 |
| 23-Aug | Job 1-3 | 1 Cor. 1:1-25 | Ps. 123 |
| 24-Aug | Job 4-6 | 1 Cor. 1:26-2:16 | Ps. 124-125 |
| 25-Aug | Job 7-9 | 1 Cor. 3 | Ps. 126-127 |
| 26-Aug | Job 10-13 | 1 Cor. 4:1-13 | Ps. 128-129 |
| 27-Aug | Job 14-16 | 1 Cor. 4:14-5:13 | Ps. 130 |
| 28-Aug | Job 17-20 | 1 Cor. 6 | Ps. 131 |
| 29-Aug | Job 21-23 | 1 Cor. 7:1-16 | Ps. 132 |
| 30-Aug | Job 24-27 | 1 Cor. 7:17-40 | Ps. 133-134 |
| 31-Aug | Job 28-30 | 1 Cor. 8 | Ps. 135 |
| 1-Sep | Job 31-33 | 1 Cor. 9:1-18 | Ps. 136:1-9 |
| 2-Sep | Job 34-36 | 1 Cor. 9:19-10:13 | Ps. 136:10-26 |
| 3-Sep | Job 37-39 | 1 Cor. 10:14-11:1 | Ps. 137 |
| 4-Sep | Job 40-42 | 1 Cor. 11:2-34 | Ps. 138 |
| 5-Sep | Eccles. 1:1-3:15 | 1 Cor. 12:1-26 | Ps. 139:1-6 |
| 6-Sep | Eccles. 3:16-6:12 | 1 Cor. 12:27-13:13 | Ps. 139:7-18 |
| 7-Sep | Eccles. 7:1-9:12 | 1 Cor. 14:1-22 | Ps. 139:19-24 |
| 8-Sep | Eccles. 9:13-12:14 | 1 Cor. 14:23-15:11 | Ps. 140:1-8 |
| 9-Sep | SS 1-4 | 1 Cor. 15:12-34 | Ps. 140:9-13 |
| 10-Sep | SS 5-8 | 1 Cor. 15:35-58 | Ps. 141 |
| 11-Sep | Isa. 1-2 | 1 Cor. 16 | Ps. 142 |
| 12-Sep | Isa. 3-5 | 2 Cor. 1:1-11 | Ps. 143:1-6 |
| 13-Sep | Isa. 6-8 | 2 Cor. 1:12-2:4 | Ps. 143:7-12 |
| 14-Sep | Isa. 9-10 | 2 Cor. 2:5-17 | Ps. 144 |
| 15-Sep | Isa. 11-13 | 2 Cor. 3 | Ps. 145 |
| 16-Sep | Isa. 14-16 | 2 Cor. 4 | Ps. 146 |
| 17-Sep | Isa. 17-19 | 2 Cor. 5 | Ps. 147:1-11 |
| 18-Sep | Isa. 20-23 | 2 Cor. 6 | Ps. 147:12-20 |
| 19-Sep | Isa. 24:1-26:19 | 2 Cor. 7 | Ps. 148 |
| 20-Sep | Isa. 26:20-28:29 | 2 Cor. 8 | Ps. 149-150 |
| 21-Sep | Isa. 29-30 | 2 Cor. 9 | Prov. 1:1-9 |

|  | | | |
|---|---|---|---|
| 22-Sep | Isa. 31-33 | 2 Cor. 10 | Prov. 1:10-22 |
| 23-Sep | Isa. 34-36 | 2 Cor. 11 | Prov. 1:23-26 |
| 24-Sep | Isa. 37-38 | 2 Cor. 12:1-10 | Prov. 1:27-33 |
| 25-Sep | Isa. 39-40 | 2 Cor. 12:11-13:14 | Prov. 2:1-15 |
| 26-Sep | Isa. 41-42 | Gal. 1 | Prov. 2:16-22 |
| 27-Sep | Isa. 43:1-44:20 | Gal. 2 | Prov. 3:1-12 |
| 28-Sep | Isa. 44:21-46:13 | Gal. 3:1-18 | Prov. 3:13-26 |
| 29-Sep | Isa. 47:1-49:13 | Gal 3:19-29 | Prov. 3:27-35 |
| 30-Sep | Isa. 49:14-51:23 | Gal 4:1-11 | Prov. 4:1-19 |
| 1-Oct | Isa. 52-54 | Gal. 4:12-31 | Prov. 4:20-27 |
| 2-Oct | Isa. 55-57 | Gal. 5 | Prov. 5:1-14 |
| 3-Oct | Isa. 58-59 | Gal. 6 | Prov. 5:15-23 |
| 4-Oct | Isa. 60-62 | Eph. 1 | Prov. 6:1-5 |
| 5-Oct | Isa. 63:1-65:16 | Eph. 2 | Prov. 6:6-19 |
| 6-Oct | Isa. 65:17-66:24 | Eph. 3:1-4:16 | Prov. 6:20-26 |
| 7-Oct | Jer. 1-2 | Eph. 4:17-32 | Prov. 6:27-35 |
| 8-Oct | Jer. 3:1-4:22 | Eph. 5 | Prov. 7:1-5 |
| 9-Oct | Jer. 4:23-5:31 | Eph. 6 | Prov. 7:6-27 |
| 10-Oct | Jer. 6:1-7:26 | Phil. 1:1-26 | Prov. 8:1-11 |
| 11-Oct | Jer. 7:26-9:16 | Phil. 1:27-2:18 | Prov. 8:12-21 |
| 12-Oct | Jer. 9:17-11:17 | Phil 2:19-30 | Prov. 8:22-36 |
| 13-Oct | Jer. 11:18-13:27 | Phil. 3 | Prov. 9:1-6 |
| 14-Oct | Jer. 14-15 | Phil. 4 | Prov. 9:7-18 |
| 15-Oct | Jer. 16-17 | Col. 1:1-23 | Prov. 10:1-5 |
| 16-Oct | Jer. 18:1-20:6 | Col. 1:24-2:15 | Prov. 10:6-14 |
| 17-Oct | Jer. 20:7-22:19 | Col. 2:16-3:4 | Prov. 10:15-26 |
| 18-Oct | Jer. 22:20-23:40 | Col. 3:5-4:1 | Prov. 10:27-32 |
| 19-Oct | Jer. 24-25 | Col. 4:2-18 | Prov. 11:1-11 |
| 20-Oct | Jer. 26-27 | 1 Thes. 1:1-2:8 | Prov. 11:12-21 |
| 21-Oct | Jer. 28-29 | 1 Thes. 2:9-3:13 | Prov. 11:22-26 |
| 22-Oct | Jer. 30:1-31:22 | 1 Thes. 4:1-5:11 | Prov. 11:27-31 |
| 23-Oct | Jer. 31:23-32:35 | 1 Thes. 5:12-28 | Prov. 12:1-14 |
| 24-Oct | Jer. 32:36-34:7 | 2 Thes. 1-2 | Prov. 12:15-20 |
| 25-Oct | Jer. 34:8-36:10 | 2 Thes. 3 | Prov. 12:21-28 |
| 26-Oct | Jer. 36:11-38:13 | 1 Tim. 1:1-17 | Prov. 13:1-4 |
| 27-Oct | Jer. 38:14-40:6 | 1 Tim. 1:18-3:13 | Prov. 13:5-13 |
| 28-Oct | Jer. 40:7-42:22 | 1 Tim. 3:14-4:10 | Prov. 13:14-21 |
| 29-Oct | Jer. 43-44 | 1 Tim. 4:11-5:16 | Prov. 13:22-25 |
| 30-Oct | Jer. 45-47 | 1 Tim. 5:17-6:21 | Prov. 14:1-6 |
| 31-Oct | Jer. 48:1-49:6 | 2 Tim. 1 | Prov. 14:7-22 |
| 1-Nov | Jer. 49:7-50:16 | 2 Tim. 2 | Prov. 14:23-27 |
| 2-Nov | Jer. 50:17-51:14 | 2 Tim. 3 | Prov. 14:28-35 |
| 3-Nov | Jer. 51:15-64 | 2 Tim. 4 | Prov. 15:1-9 |
| 4-Nov | Jer. 52-Lam. 1 | Ti. 1:1-9 | Prov. 15:10-17 |
| 5-Nov | Lam. 2:1-3:38 | Ti. 1:10-2:15 | Prov. 15:18-26 |
| 6-Nov | Lam. 3:39-5:22 | Ti. 3 | Prov. 15:27-33 |
| 7-Nov | Ezek. 1:1-3:21 | Philemon 1 | Prov. 16:1-9 |
| 8-Nov | Ezek. 3:22-5:17 | Heb. 1:1-2:4 | Prov. 16:10-21 |
| 9-Nov | Ezek. 6-7 | Heb. 2:5-18 | Prov. 16:22-33 |
| 10-Nov | Ezek. 8-10 | Heb. 3:1-4:3 | Prov. 17:1-5 |
| 11-Nov | Ezek. 11-12 | Heb. 4:4-5:10 | Prov. 17:6-12 |
| 12-Nov | Ezek. 13-14 | Heb. 5:11-6:20 | Prov. 17:13-22 |
| 13-Nov | Ezek. 15:1-16:43 | Heb. 7:1-28 | Prov. 17:23-28 |
| 14-Nov | Ezek. 16:44-17:24 | Heb. 8:1-9:10 | Prov. 18:1-7 |

| | | | |
|---|---|---|---|
| 15-Nov | Ezek. 18-19 | Heb. 9:11-28 | Prov. 18:8-17 |
| 16-Nov | Ezek. 20 | Heb. 10:1-25 | Prov. 18:18-24 |
| 17-Nov | Ezek. 21-22 | Heb. 10:26-39 | Prov. 19:1-8 |
| 18-Nov | Ezek. 23 | Heb. 11:1-31 | Prov. 19:9-14 |
| 19-Nov | Ezek. 24-26 | Heb. 11:32-40 | Prov. 19:15-21 |
| 20-Nov | Ezek. 27-28 | Heb. 12:1-13 | Prov. 19:22-29 |
| 21-Nov | Ezek. 29-30 | Heb. 12:14-29 | Prov. 20:1-18 |
| 22-Nov | Ezek. 31-32 | Heb. 13 | Prov. 20:19-24 |
| 23-Nov | Ezek. 33:1-34:10 | Jas. 1 | Prov. 20:25-30 |
| 24-Nov | Ezek. 34:11-36:15 | Jas. 2 | Prov. 21:1-8 |
| 25-Nov | Ezek. 36:16-37:28 | Jas. 3 | Prov. 21:9-18 |
| 26-Nov | Ezek. 38-39 | Jas. 4:1-5:6 | Prov. 21:19-24 |
| 27-Nov | Ezek. 40 | Jas. 5:7-20 | Prov. 21:25-31 |
| 28-Nov | Ezek. 41:1-43:12 | 1 Pet. 1:1-12 | Prov. 22:1-9 |
| 29-Nov | Ezek. 43:13-44:31 | 1 Pet. 1:13-2:3 | Prov. 22:10-23 |
| 30-Nov | Ezek. 45-46 | 1 Pet. 2:4-17 | Prov. 22:24-29 |
| 1-Dec | Ezek. 47-48 | 1 Pet. 2:18-3:7 | Prov. 23:1-9 |
| 2-Dec | Dan. 1:1-2:23 | 1 Pet. 3:8-4:19 | Prov. 23:10-16 |
| 3-Dec | Dan. 2:24-3:30 | 1 Pet. 5 | Prov. 23:17-25 |
| 4-Dec | Dan. 4 | 2 Pet. 1 | Prov. 23:26-35 |
| 5-Dec | Dan. 5 | 2 Pet. 2 | Prov. 24:1-18 |
| 6-Dec | Dan. 6:1-7:14 | 2 Pet. 3 | Prov. 24:19-27 |
| 7-Dec | Dan. 7:15-8:27 | 1 John 1:1-2:17 | Prov. 24:28-34 |
| 8-Dec | Dan. 9-10 | 1 John 2:18-29 | Prov. 25:1-12 |
| 9-Dec | Dan. 11-12 | 1 John 3:1-12 | Prov. 25:13-17 |
| 10-Dec | Hos. 1-3 | 1 John 3:13-4:16 | Prov. 25:18-28 |
| 11-Dec | Hos. 4-6 | 1 John 4:17-5:21 | Prov. 26:1-16 |
| 12-Dec | Hos. 7-10 | 2 John | Prov. 26:17-21 |
| 13-Dec | Hos. 11-14 | 3 John | Prov. 26:22-27:9 |
| 14-Dec | Joel 1:1-2:17 | Jude | Prov. 27:10-17 |
| 15-Dec | Joel 2:18-3:21 | Rev. 1:1-2:11 | Prov. 27:18-27 |
| 16-Dec | Amos 1:1-4:5 | Rev. 2:12-29 | Prov. 28:1-8 |
| 17-Dec | Amos 4:6-6:14 | Rev. 3 | Prov. 28:9-16 |
| 18-Dec | Amos 7-9 | Rev. 4:1-5:5 | Prov. 28:17-24 |
| 19-Dec | Obad-Jonah | Rev. 5:6-14 | Prov. 28:25-28 |
| 20-Dec | Mic. 1:1-4:5 | Rev. 6:1-7:8 | Prov. 29:1-8 |
| 21-Dec | Mic. 4:6-7:20 | Rev. 7:9-8:13 | Prov. 29:9-14 |
| 22-Dec | Nah. 1-3 | Rev. 9-10 | Prov. 29:15-23 |
| 23-Dec | Hab. 1-3 | Rev. 11 | Prov. 29:24-27 |
| 24-Dec | Zeph. 1-3 | Rev. 12 | Prov. 30:1-6 |
| 25-Dec | Hag. 1-2 | Rev. 13:1-14:13 | Prov. 30:7-16 |
| 26-Dec | Zech. 1-4 | Rev. 14:14-16:3 | Prov. 30:17-20 |
| 27-Dec | Zech. 5-8 | Rev. 16:4-21 | Prov. 30:21-28 |
| 28-Dec | Zech. 9-11 | Rev. 17:1-18:8 | Prov. 30:29-33 |
| 29-Dec | Zech. 12-14 | Rev. 18:9-24 | Prov. 31:1-9 |
| 30-Dec | Mal. 1-2 | Rev. 19-20 | Prov. 31:10-17 |
| 31-Dec | Mal. 3-4 | Rev. 21-22 | Prov. 31:18-31 |